AF291380

ICONIC SABRINA

THE MAKING OF A LEGEND IN 50 IMAGES

The unauthorized collection

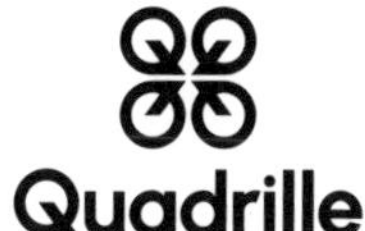

Quadrille

'I LITERALLY GET TO SING INTO A MICROPHONE. THAT'S MY JOB. IT'S EVERYTHING I'VE ALWAYS WANTED.'[1]

INTRODUCTION

You'd have to have been living under a rock for the last couple of years in order not to know who Sabrina Carpenter is. With her tiny stature, tumbling blonde curls and cheeky smile, Sabrina has captured the hearts of fans all over the world – and kept us all in fits of giggles into the bargain.

From her beginnings as a ten-year-old girl singing covers on YouTube to her current life as a Grammy-winning superstar selling out arenas, Sabrina has been on an incredible journey. Perhaps you grew up watching her portray Maya Hart on the Disney Channel's *Girl Meets World*; maybe your first experience of her was when she shot to international fame with the summer-defining earworm that is 'Espresso'. Regardless, there's no denying that Sabrina Carpenter is something very special indeed.

She's toured with Taylor Swift and Ariana Grande, counts Coldplay, Katy Perry and Adele among her fans, and is credited with sparking a return to old-fashioned Hollywood glamour – and she's done it all with a spring in her step, a smile on her face and more than a little innuendo. So buckle up, down a shot of espresso and get yourself glammed up – it's Sabrina Carpenter time.

GIRL MEETS WORLD

A child star in Pennsylvania.

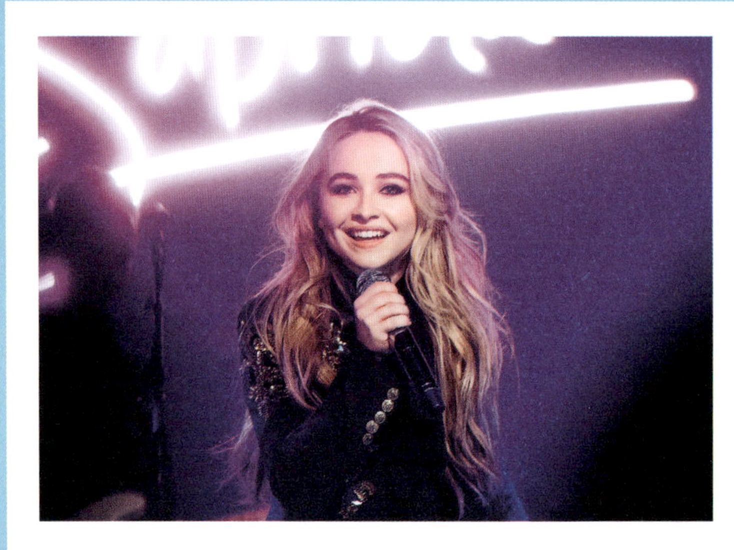

'I'M A TAURUS, AND I THINK
THAT MIGHT HAVE SOMETHING
TO DO WITH THE FACT THAT
I'VE ALWAYS JUST BEEN VERY
DRIVEN. SOME PEOPLE LIKE
TO CALL IT STUBBORN.
I LIKE TO SAY DRIVEN.'[2]

AN ICON IS BORN

'I have three older sisters, and I'm the baby. So that's why I'm an asshole.' [3]

Sabrina Carpenter was born on 11 May 1999 in Quakertown, Pennsylvania, and grew up in East Greenville with her parents David, who works for an X-ray company, and Elizabeth, a chiropractor, as well as three sisters, Sarah, Cayla and Shannon.

In an interview with *Vogue*, Sabrina described her hometown as: 'Desolate […] So I had a really big imagination, which was necessary for me, I guess!' [4]

That big imagination was matched by a big talent for singing and acting. In 2024, she told *W Magazine*: 'I can't even remember when I started singing and performing and entertaining because I was really, really little.' [5]

One of her earliest forays into performing came when her family used to eat at an Irish pub called the Limeport Inn, and a waitress would take Sabrina to other tables to sing 'Happy Birthday'. Some customers paid her, though her mum made her give the money back. 'That was a short-lived dream, but also kind of my first real audience!' [6]

At the age of six, she took part in a school talent show, singing 'Part of Your World' and wearing a *Little Mermaid* costume. 'I liked it because it was a crop top and I felt edgy … at *six*.' [7]

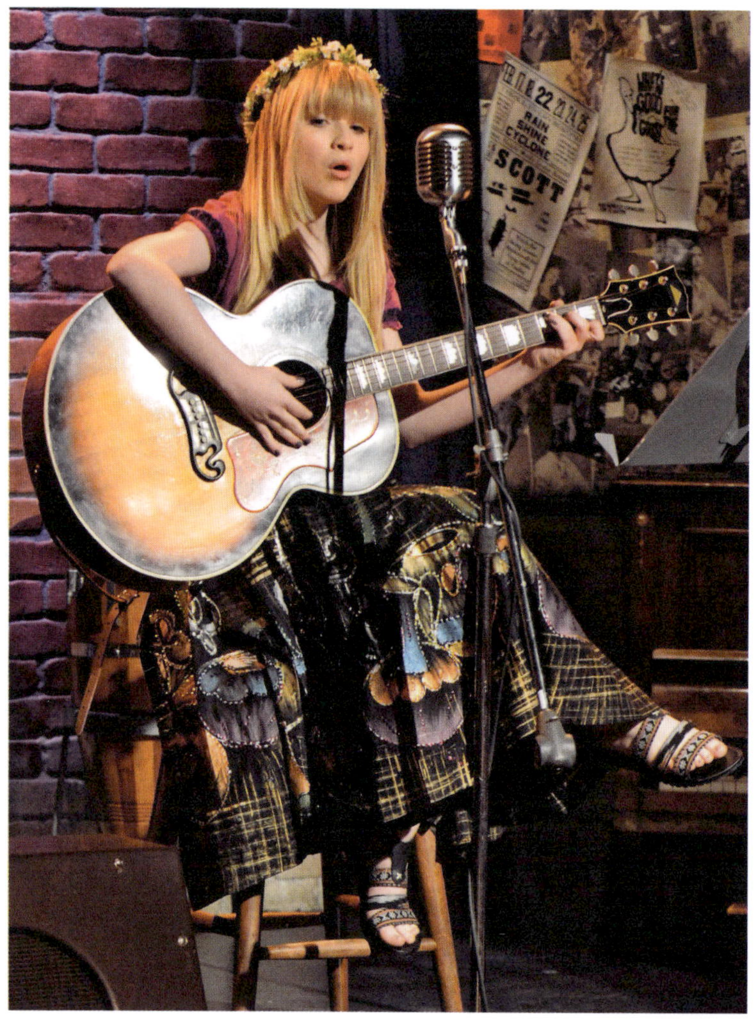
RAIN
SHINE
CYCLONE
SCOTT

SABRINA SUPERSTAR

Sabrina started home-schooling when she reached the fourth grade, and at the age of ten she took part in the Mileyworld Superstar competition, a contest for fans of the singer Miley Cyrus. Despite her very young age, Sabrina made it into the top three, and impressed voters with performances of songs including 'Makes Me Wanna Pray' by Christina Aguilera and 'Hoedown Throwdown' by Miley herself.

The contest further ignited a spark that had already been simmering. Speaking to *Vogue*, Sabrina said: 'After that contest ended – did not win, got to meet Miley, though, big perk – I kept doing it because I just loved it so much. I also felt like I was finding my voice through covering other people's songs.'[8]

Her dad turned a cupboard into a recording space for her: 'It was like a Harry Potter closet under the staircase. He painted it purple and put padding on the walls for me and [I had] my microphone in there. And I just felt super legit.'[9]

Her parents supported her, but all the ambition and drive came from Sabrina herself: 'When I was younger a lot of people assumed it was my parents' dream that they were trying to fulfil through me, and I always had to tell people it really had nothing to do with anyone but my 11-year-old self.'[10]

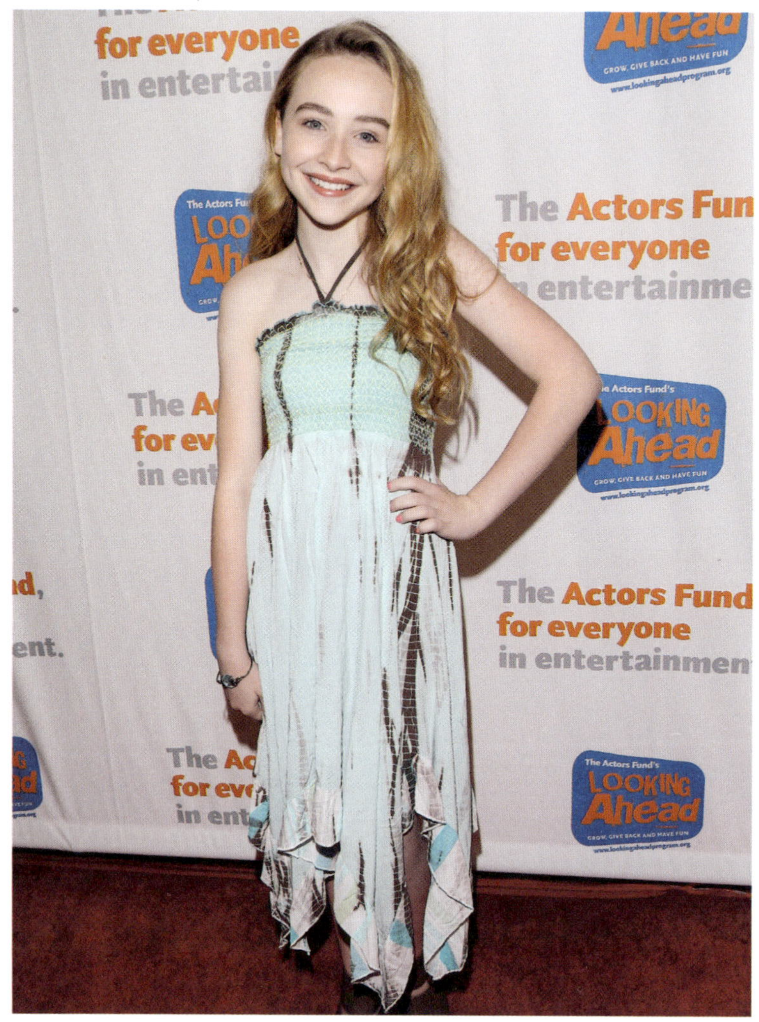
Ahead
GROW, GIVE BACK AND HAVE FUN
www.lookingaheadprogram.org
for everyone
in entertainme
The Actors Fund
for everyone
in entertainme
The Actors Fund's
LOOKING
Ahead
GROW, GIVE BACK AND HAVE FUN
www.lookingaheadprogram.org
The Actors Fund
for everyone
in entertainmen
The Actors Fund's
Looking
Ahead
GROW, GIVE BACK AND HAVE FUN
www.lookingaheadprogram.org

HITTING THE SMALL SCREEN

'I was always performing as a child; anytime there was a stage, or an elevated hill I could pretend was a stage, I was straight to it.' [11]

As well as singing, the young Sabrina loved acting, and she landed her very first TV role in 2011. Although she had already developed the playful sense of humour that her fans would later come to know and love – '[I was] a sarcastic, snarky kid from day one,' she told *Vogue* [12] – her first role was a serious one, as she appeared on *Law & Order: Special Victims Unit*. In a later interview, she explained: 'I was thrown off by that booking because I always wanted to do comedy. And on that show, I was [playing] a victim. I remember running lines with my dad and asking: "Is this what acting is?"' [13]

This was soon followed by a role as a mean girl in an episode of popular Netflix drama *Orange is the New Black*.

STEPPING INTO THE SPOTLIGHT

Although she continued singing (in 2012, she appeared on the compilation album *Disney Fairies: Faith, Trust and Pixie Dust*, alongside fellow future superstars Zendaya and Selena Gomez), Sabrina kept up with her acting career. In 2013, she secured a lead role in the Disney Channel sitcom *Girl Meets World* playing Maya Hart, whom she later described as: 'Very witty, very quick. Kind of emotional and all over the place, which feels like me in lots of ways.'[14]

Sabrina and her mum moved to LA for filming, and the show ran until 2017. As an adult, Sabrina has reflected on the challenges of progressing from a child star to an adult pop sensation, as sometimes people struggle to accept that she has grown up. As she told *Variety*: 'I'm 900 inappropriate jokes away from being a Disney actor, but people still see me that way. I'm always extremely flattered to be grouped in with the other women and girls who I've idolised and looked up to who came from that, but I feel very distant from it.'[15]

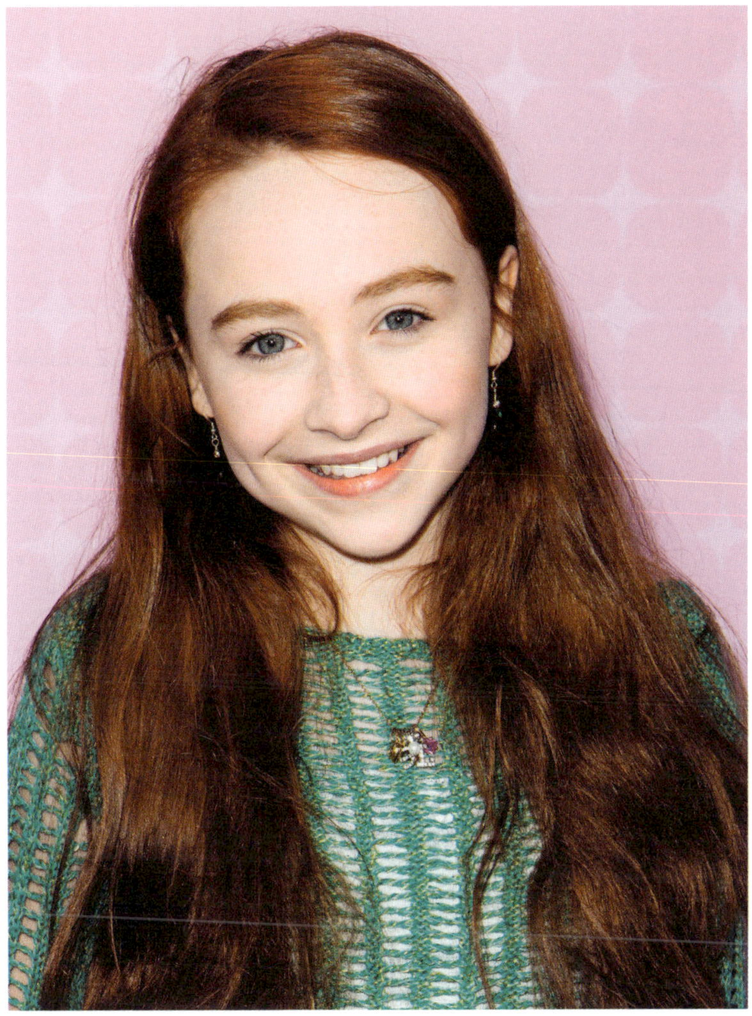

CAN'T BLAME A GIRL FOR TRYING

'Music was always the thing as a child that made me feel like I understood more about life.' [16]

In 2014 – at the age of just 14 – Sabrina signed a five-record deal with Hollywood Records. Her first EP, *Can't Blame a Girl for Trying,* was released in April that year, and was followed by her 2015 debut album, *Eyes Wide Open.*

The following year, Sabrina performed at Bethlehem Musikfest in her home state of Pennsylvania – a festival she had attended herself many times before. 'This is so surreal for me,' she told the crowd. '[…] I grew up seeing some of my favourite artists here. This time I'm onstage looking at all of you and it's really weird.'[17]

Although she was beginning to realise her dreams, Sabrina was still a way off from the level of stardom she's achieved today, and has since shared that in the decade it took for her music to really break through into the mainstream, she took a few wrong turns – but she's grateful for them. She told *Time* magazine: 'For a long time I was constantly guided and misguided. I'm so grateful for all those times where I was led astray, because now I'm a lot more equipped going into situations where I have to trust my own instincts.'[18]

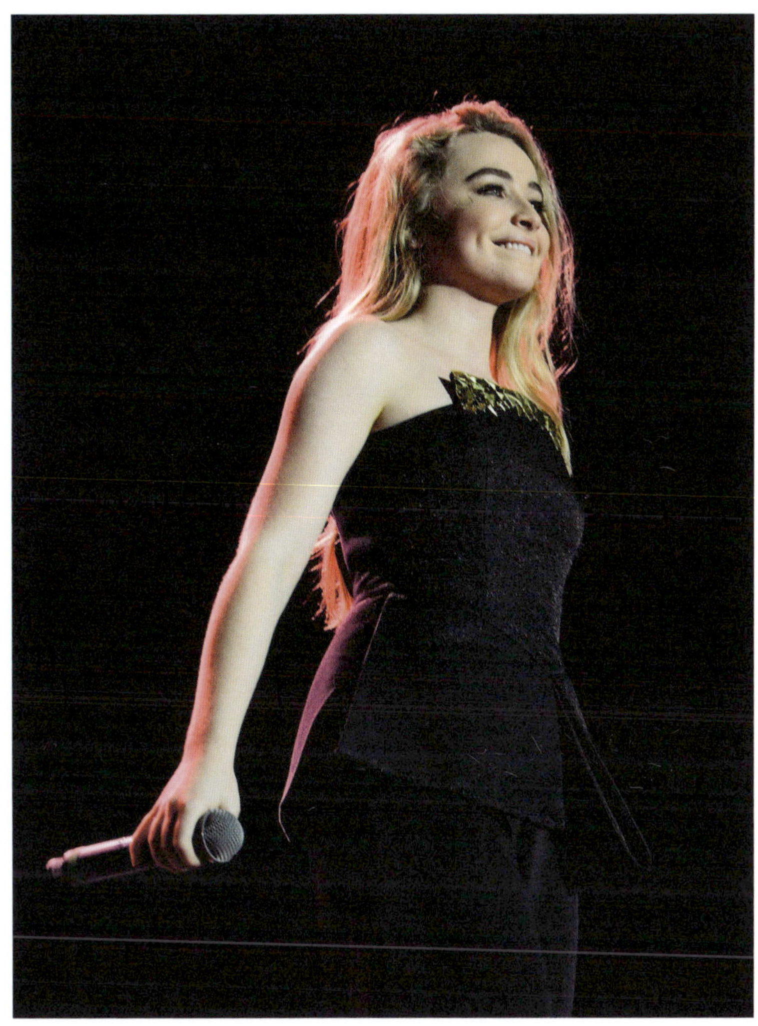

EVOLUTION

Growing up and finding her sound.

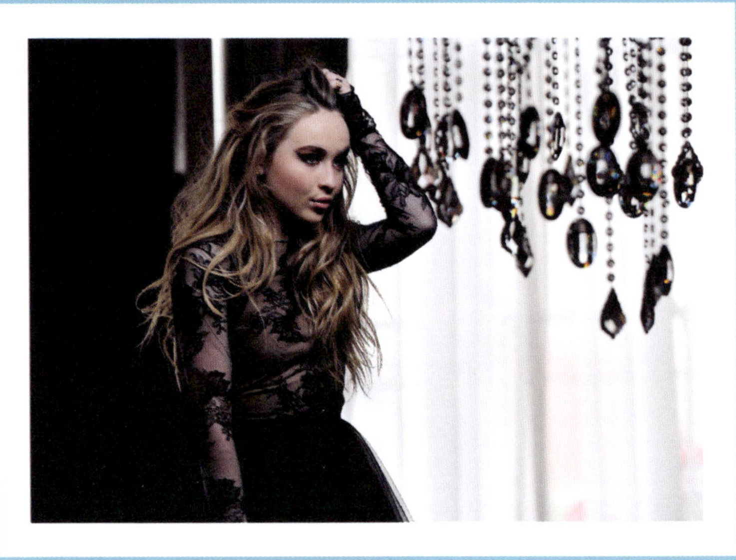

'I NEVER HAD THE PLAN B, AND IT WASN'T EVEN A THOUGHT IN MY MIND THAT IT WOULDN'T WORK OUT. I JUST ALWAYS KNEW IT WAS ABOUT NOT IF IT WOULD HAPPEN BUT WHEN IT WOULD HAPPEN'[19]

THUMBS, HANDS AND A STEP TOWARDS THE FUTURE

In October 2016, Sabrina released her second album, *EVOlution*, which marked a step away from the teen pop/folky sound of her earlier music, moving towards a more dance- and electropop-focused vibe. The album's standout track was probably 'Thumbs', the video for which showed Sabrina dancing in a subway car, echoing the opening episode of *Girl Meets World* and demonstrating just how far she had come. Despite the song's lyrics, Sabrina could certainly never be accused of twiddling *her* thumbs – she got straight on the road to promote the album with her first ever headline tour, starting in Nashville, Tennessee, and finishing in Milan, Italy.

At around this time, Sabrina also featured on the single 'Hands' with UK band The Vamps and Swedish DJ Mike Perry. This song may go down in history as the first time the young singer had sworn on a record – although it was an accident. She'd never seen the lyrics written down, and had instead learned them from listening to the demo, so she didn't realise it was supposed to be 'leave your *shirt* at the door'. Oops.

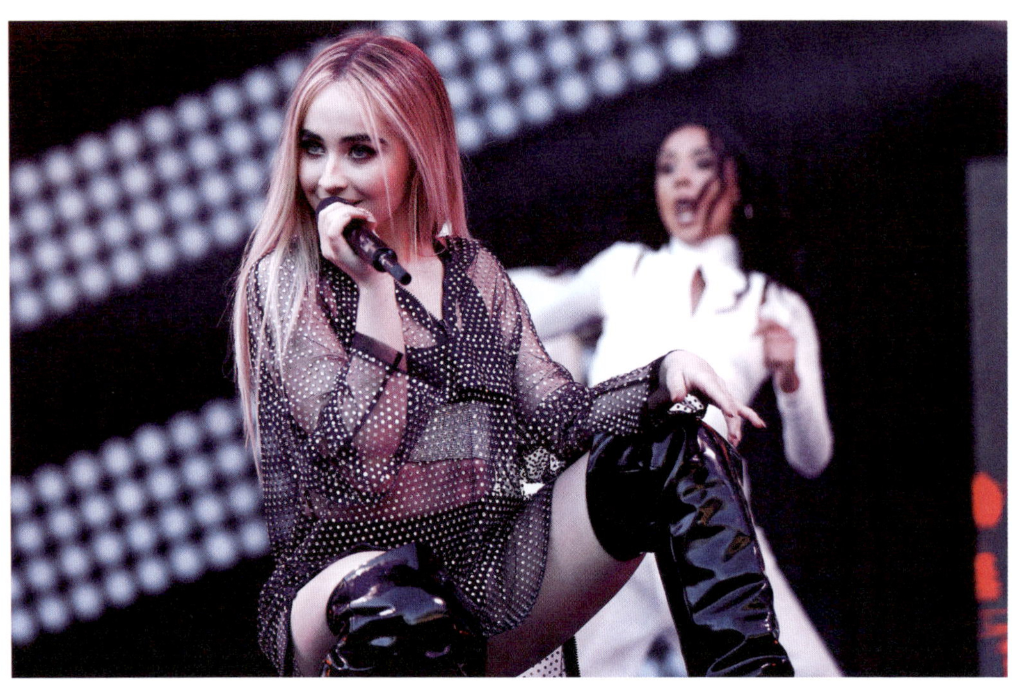

DANGEROUS WOMEN

On 29 June and 1 July 2017, the worlds of Nickelodeon and Disney collided when Sabrina performed as the opening act for Ariana Grande at the Brazilian shows for Ariana's Dangerous Woman tour.

In an interview a few weeks later, Sabrina reflected on the experience: 'I mean, her fans are already incredible, but then put Brazil into the picture [and] I've never seen such a crowd. It was incredible. She was amazing – and the whole show was beautiful.'

Perhaps it was a sign of things to come – six years later, she'd return to Brazil as part of Taylor Swift's Eras tour (see page 46).

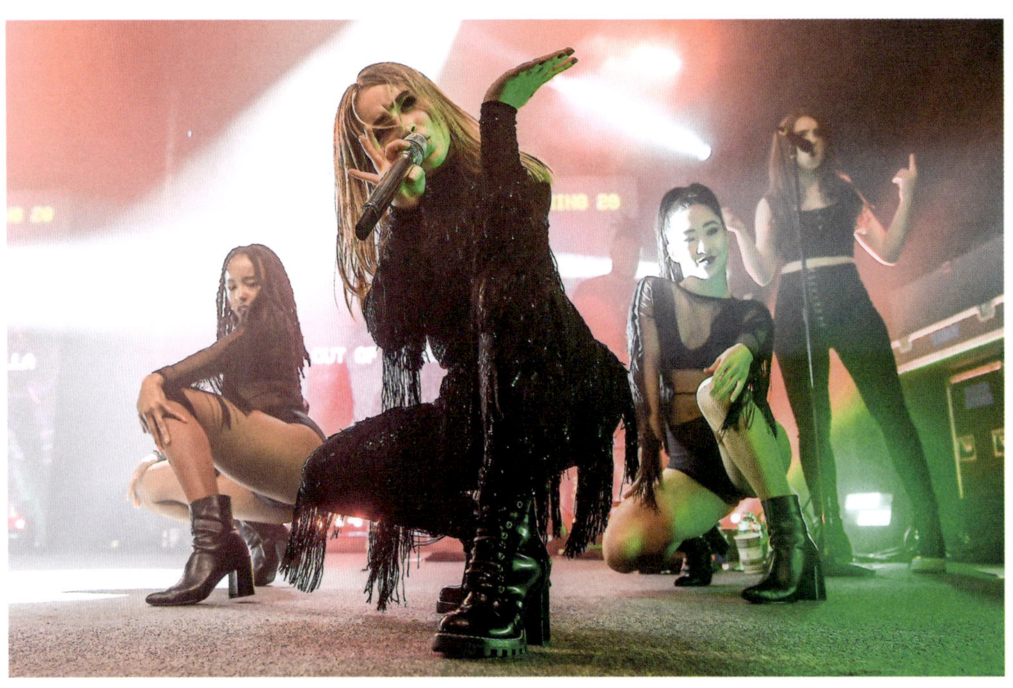

SINGULARLY SABRINA

'My advice to my younger self is: don't take other people's opinions more seriously than your own.' [20]

Sabrina was committed to her time in the studio, and November 2018 saw the release of her third album, *Singular: Act I*, which she promoted with a tour in March 2019 across the US, Canada and parts of Asia. It was quickly followed by *Singular: Act II* in July 2019.

Singular: Act I features the song 'Sue Me', which she wrote when she was being sued by her former managers. 'I was freshly 18,' she later explained to the *Guardian*. 'That was like, oop! I don't even know what to do with that.' [21]

Her decision to channel a stressful situation into a cheeky and playful song gave fans an early taste of the bold, tongue-in-cheek attitude that would soon become her trademark. She told *Vogue*: 'I'm so happy that [the song] exists because I think that when a lot of people try to figure out where maybe my personality and my music and the bluntness and the honesty come from, I do think it started in that chapter of my life.' [22]

'Sue Me' was accompanied by a video featuring Sabrina and her friend (and *Kissing Booth* star) Joey King.

SILVER SCREEN

As her albums kept piling up, Sabrina was also building up her film credits. In 2018 she appeared in the hard-hitting *The Hate U Give*, based on the book by Angie Thomas, taking on the challenging role of Hailey, initially one of the closest friends of the film's protagonist, Starr. As the film progresses, Hailey fails to understand the racism Starr is experiencing, and the ways in which she herself is complicit in it. Reflecting on the role, Sabrina said: 'The reaction has been so interesting because people have been like, "I really wanna say good job but also I don't want people to know that I know you." That kind of reaction is great because it means that I did what I had to do. As much as it's not a role that people like, it's unfortunately a role that helps you understand why the movie was made.'[23]

In September 2019, she played an altogether more lovable character, appearing as the pint-sized older sister to the title character in *Tall Girl*. Although it was a supporting role, her sparky portrayal of beauty queen Harper somewhat stole the show.

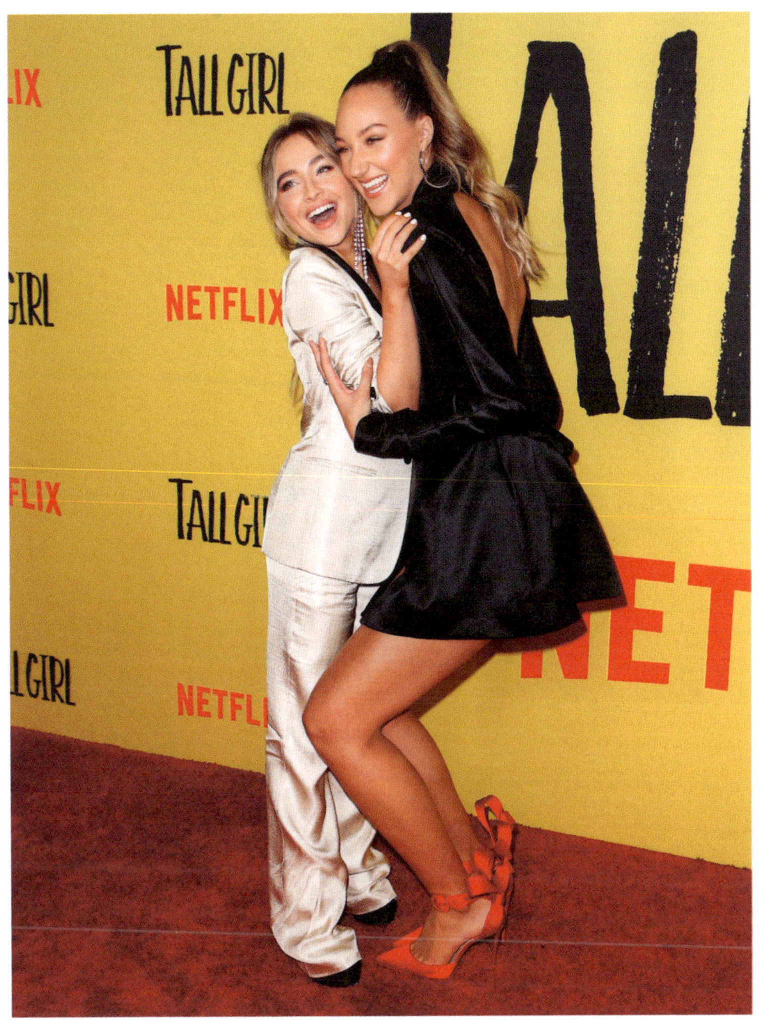

YOU CAN'T SIT WITH US

March 2020 saw Sabrina make her Broadway debut as Cady Heron in the musical *Mean Girls* – but devastatingly, the show's run was cut short due to the COVID-19 pandemic. Sabrina later told CBS: 'I rehearsed for about three months in New York, and we opened our first two nights, and then COVID humbled me – humbled me very quickly! Like, I was sent home and was just like, "Wow, I feel I could do eight shows a week, you know, and I've been training for it. And now it's just, like, silence."'[24]

Everyone who lived through those strange and stressful lockdown years will relate to this sense of the world being thrown off-course, but the era also marked a distinct coming-of-age period for Sabrina as an artist. As she explained to *Variety*: 'For the people who love [my] early records and listen to them, I love you. But I personally feel a sense of separation from them, largely due to a shift in who I am as a person and artist, pre-pandemic and post-pandemic.'[25]

Something big was coming.

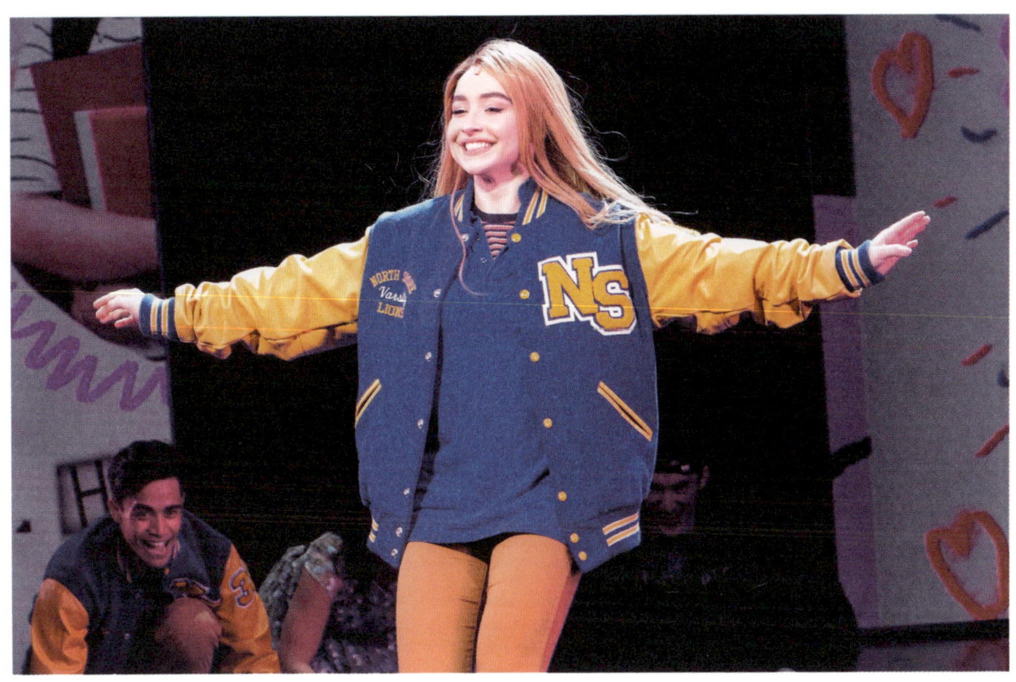

FAST TIMES AND FAST NIGHTS

The world begins to sit up and pay attention.

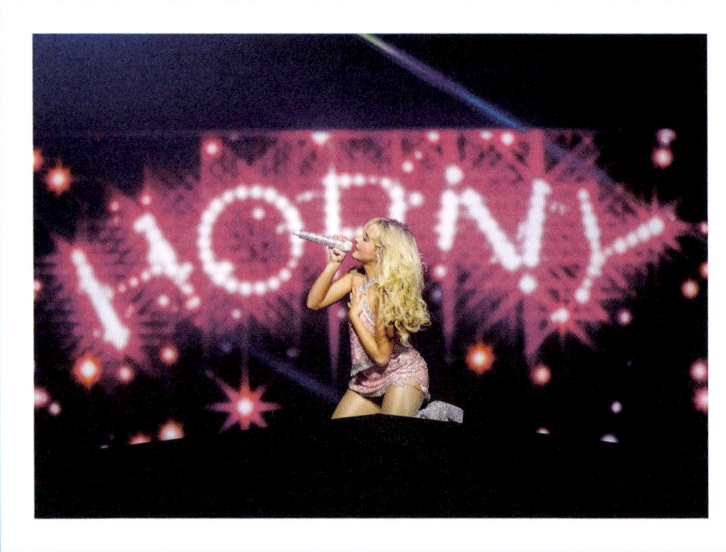

'IF YOU WANT TO CALL ME A POLLY POCKET, A BRATZ DOLL, I DON'T CARE. YOU'LL MEET ME AND THEN YOU'LL BE LIKE, DAMN, SHE TALKS A LOT MORE THAN THE DOLLS DO.'[26]

SKIN IN THE GAME

On 22 January 2021 – after leaving Hollywood Records (after four albums, not five) and moving to Island Records – Sabrina released the single 'Skin'. The song is thought by some fans to be a reference to Olivia Rodrigo's 'Driver's License', which was rumoured to be about a love triangle between Sabrina, Olivia and Joshua Bassett. However, Sabrina has always refused to be drawn into gossip about her song or the situation, telling *W Magazine*: 'I get why people are interested. But they can listen to my album and decide for themselves what the songs are about.'[27]

The song marked Sabrina's first entry into the Billboard Hot 100, hitting number 48, and was accompanied by a striking video showing Sabrina and actor Gavin Leatherwood (best known for his role in *The Chilling Adventures of Sabrina* – geddit?) as a couple enjoying their lives together despite the storms and events around them. We see them sharing a romantic dinner while attempting to ignore an earthquake, sitting on a sofa while rain drenches them, and lying on a bed as they're buried in a blanket of snow. Whatever the song is truly about, both it and the video send a powerful message about rising above controversy and criticism.

'[My songs are] my diary. Once I put it out there, it's for other people to interpret. I try not to tell people what a song is explicitly about. People don't always know what's going on inside the minds of anyone, let along [that of] a young girl who's navigating love and a lot of things for the first time.' [28]

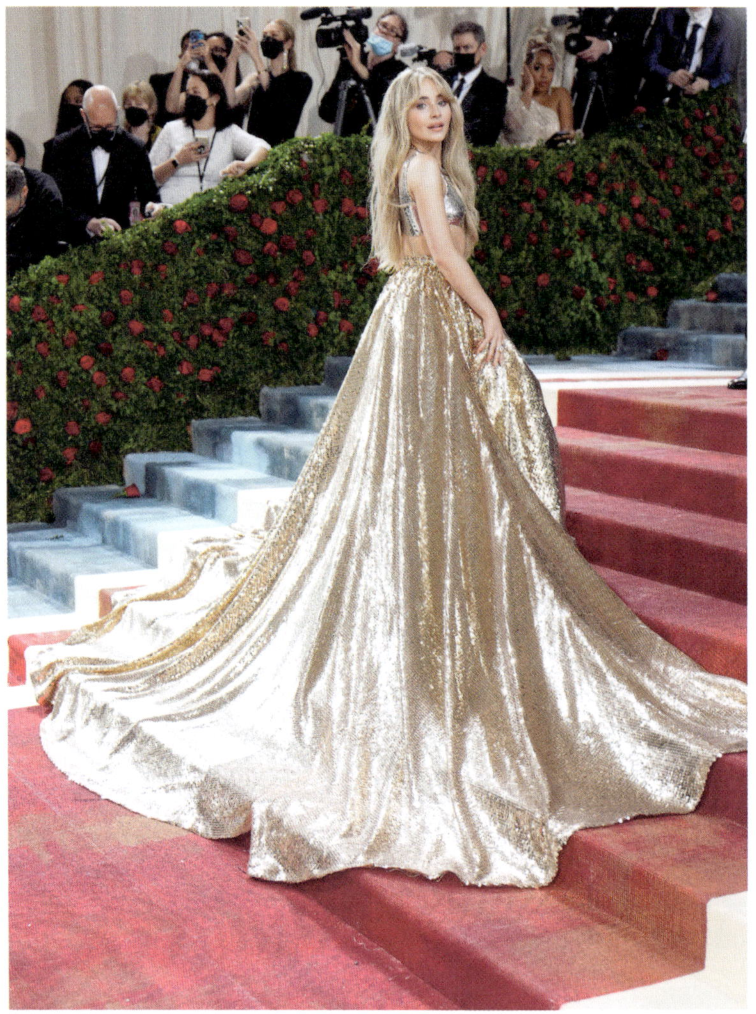

GILDED GLAMOUR

May 2022 saw Sabrina attend her first ever Met Gala, wowing onlookers in a shimmering silver top and a flowing golden sequinned skirt that had been custom-made for her by designer Julien Dossena at Paco Rabanne. The Met Gala is widely considered the highlight of the fashion year, with celebrities donning stunning haute couture outfits based around specific themes. The theme for 2022 was widely described as 'Gilded Glamour' – and Sabrina more than delivered.

Speaking to *Vogue* about the event, Sabrina said: 'To me, [the Met Gala] is the Super Bowl. I love seeing so many incredible people come together under one roof for art and fashion.'[29]

She was slightly less eloquent when speaking to Emma Chamberlain on the red carpet at the event: 'This is my first time, so I'm peeing myself.'[30]

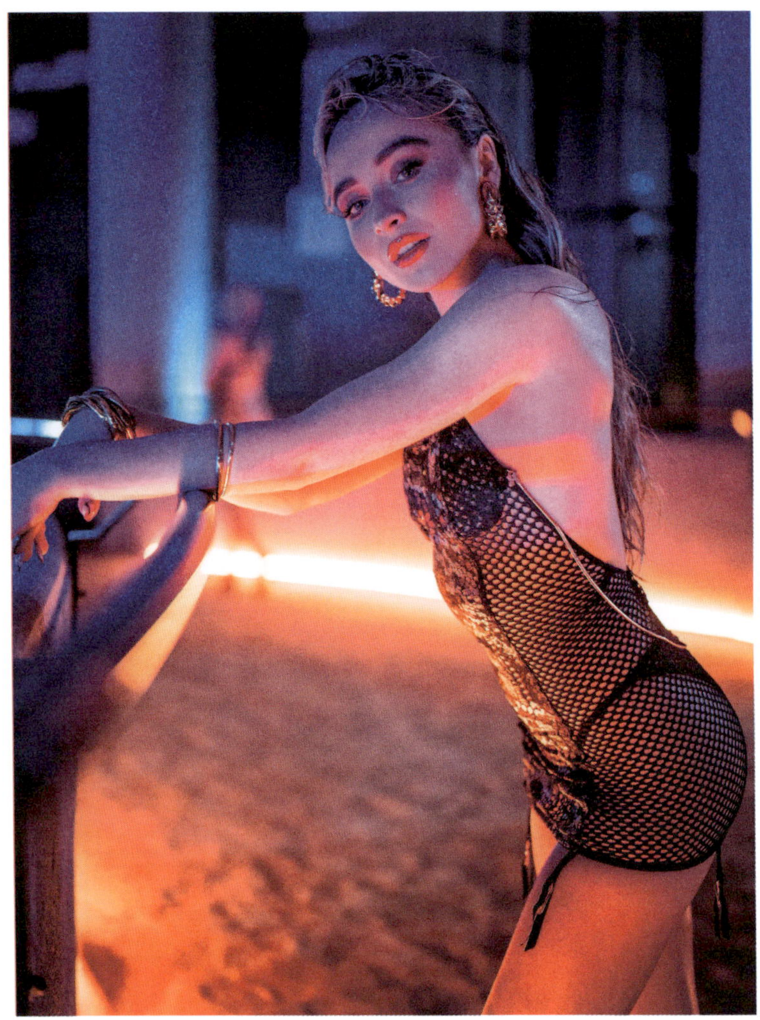

EMAILS I CAN'T SEND

'[In your twenties,] everything's happening for the first time, meaning all the lows feel even lower and the highs feel even higher. But it's all happening at such an accelerated speed. So the album, for me, was really a time capsule of a special time in my life when I dealt with many things for the first time.' [31]

On 15 July 2022, Sabrina released *Emails I Can't Send*, her fifth studio album – but, she told *Vogue*, 'my first big-girl album'. [32] It reached number 23 on the US Billboard 200 chart. The album title struck a chord with many people – after all, who hasn't written an email or text to get all their feelings out, while knowing they'll never really be able to send it? In an interview, Sabrina explained: 'I wrote most of the songs on *Emails I Can't Send* not intending to ever put them out in the world, because I don't think I would have written those songs if [I'd] thought about other people hearing them.' [33] The album inspired fans to share their own unsent emails in fan forums. [34]

Explaining how important this album is to her, Sabrina told *Glamour*: 'It's not that [my earlier] albums were throwaways for me, but they were definitely me not really knowing who I was yet. [...] So I look at this album as a first album for me in many ways.' [35]

TOUR TIME

Sabrina supported her new album with a world tour, which started in September 2022 and ended in August 2023. There were 80 tour dates, spanning four continents, and the initial US leg of the tour sold out in less than a day.

Writing on Instagram, Sabrina said: 'u sold out the whole emails i can't send tour in less than a day!!!!!! This is insane and i couldn't be more grateful. i've pictured playing these songs live since the day i wrote them, so i promise to give you an indelible night where you can sing and dance and forget he isn't texting u back!!'[36]

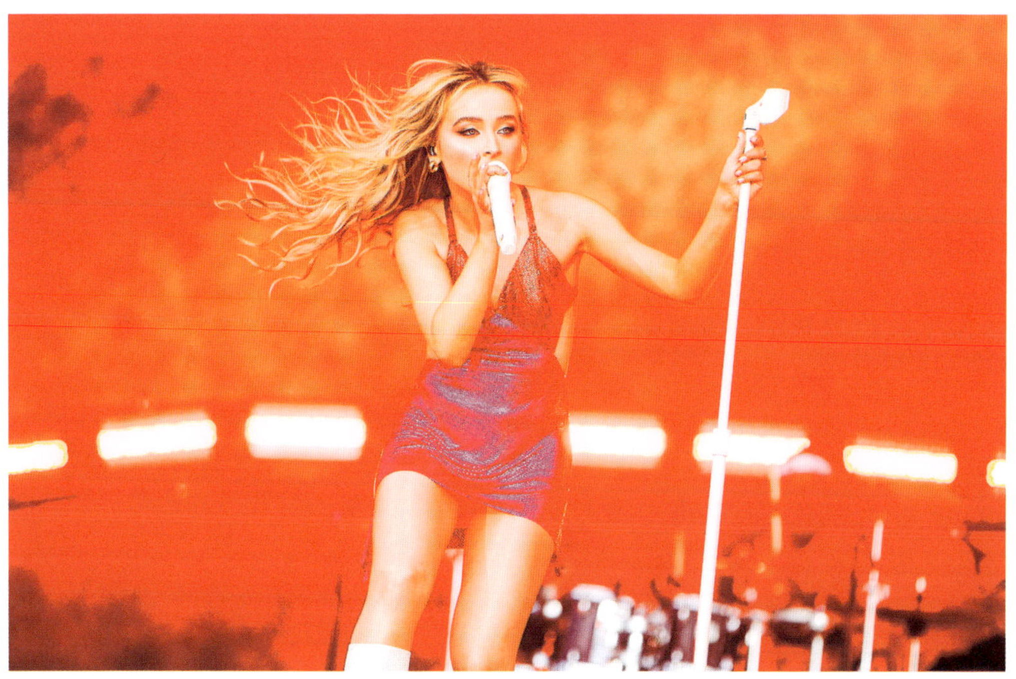

THE STYLE EVOLUTION OF SABRINA CARPENTER

'I started wearing outfits that felt more like myself. And then it sort of bled into these songs that felt more and more like my personality.' [37]

While *Emails* marked a turning point in terms of Sabrina finding her own sound, it was also at around this time that she really came into her own in terms of fashion. With her profile growing and the tour gathering pace, Sabrina's style started to get noticed by fans and media alike. Her signature look, which has become known as 'Brinacore', pairs old Hollywood bombshell glamour with a dash of Y2K-style cheekiness: think sparkly mini dresses and corsets with stockings and dizzyingly high go-go boots.

She told *Glamour*: 'I have so much respect for fashion. I feel like I've grown up around it, and it's such a big part of what I do. I'm a mess if I don't wear things I feel confident in. Performing is so vulnerable that if you don't feel 100 per cent good about what you're in, it's really hard to do it fearlessly.' [38]

In another interview with *Time*, she explained: 'Femininity is something that I've always embraced. And if right now that means corsets and garter belts and fuzzy robes or whatever […], then that's what that means.' [39]

Not everyone is as taken with the look as her fans, however. '[You'll] still get the occasional mother that has a strong opinion on how you should be dressing. And to that I just say, don't come to the show, and that's OK.' [40]

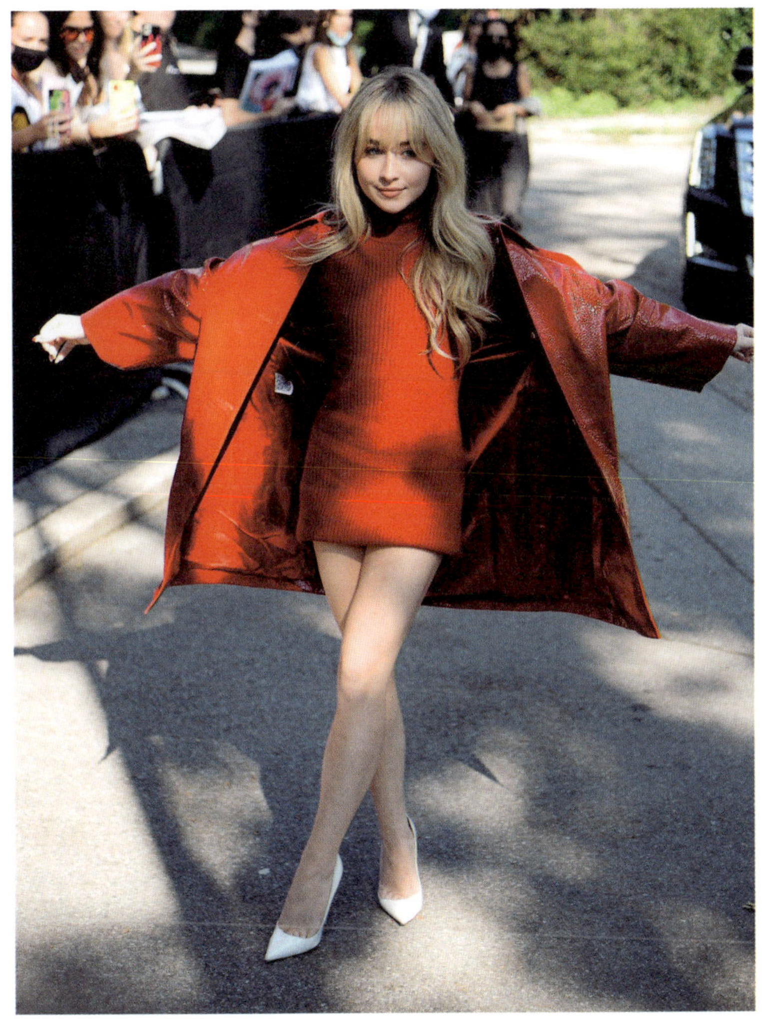

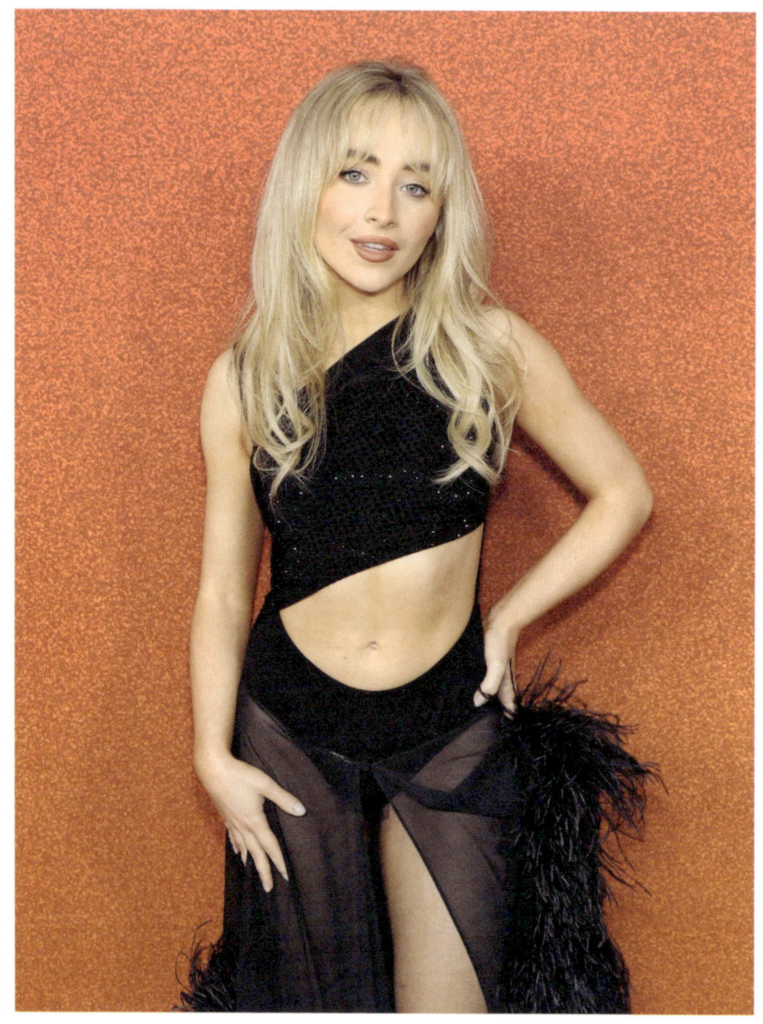

THE COFFEE'S BREWING ...

During a short break from the Emails tour, Sabrina started writing the album that would eventually become *Short n' Sweet*. She was staying in a small town in France called Chailland, and invited songwriters Amy Allen, John Ryan and Julian Bunetta to join her.

She told *Vogue*: 'When I tell you it was a ghost town – all there was was this house, an empty church, and then like five minutes up the road was a creperie. [...] I would write for a bit, I would start something, and then I would go on a walk, and I would get an espresso from the creperie.'[41]

An espresso, you say? That's right – something about that little daily shot of caffeine seemed to spark an idea, and Sabrina started working on what was to become her greatest hit to date. In an interview with the *Guardian*, she later explained: '[When I started writing "Espresso"], it was a manifestation tactic, because no one liked me romantically at that point – no one was obsessed with me. I didn't have anyone I was even talking to. I've always been a bit delusional in that sense.'[42]

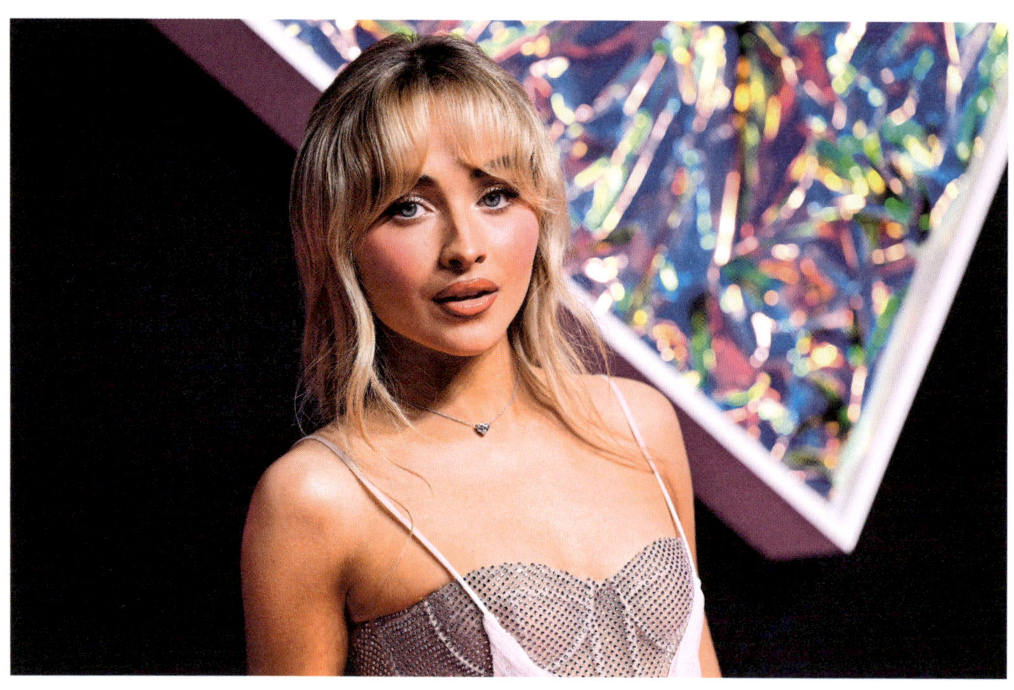

NONSENSE

There was one song in particular on *Emails I Can't Send* that quickly became a fan favourite: 'Nonsense'. While much of the album is deeply personal and concerned with heartache, 'Nonsense' is undeniably, joyously silly. Sabrina told *Vogue*: 'The whole album's a heartbreak album, and then "Nonsense" is sort of like: *Maybe I could fall in love again*. It's a very funny, unserious song.'[43]

The song was released as a single on 14 November 2022, accompanied by a music video. Sabrina announced the video on her Instagram, with the caption playing on her fondness for performing different outros to the song live (more on this on page 48):

'bc i read all your concerns and comments
i made a music video for nonsense
my love interest is so hot it's obnoxious
i think there's a banana in his pocket
at 9:30 go click the link and watch it'[44]

The video shows Sabrina and two friends getting ready for a party, where they meet some cute boys. The obnoxiously hot love interest mentioned above certainly steals the show – though some might argue that he looks suspiciously like Sabrina wearing a 'Dipshit' baseball cap.

TAYBRINA

'To work with someone [who] cares about you as a person as well as an artist … That's been the biggest gift.' [45]

After spending the rest of 2022 and the first half of 2023 on her epic Emails I Can't Send tour, Sabrina had even more exciting news to share. In June 2023, she announced that she would be the opening act for Taylor Swift's Eras tour in Latin America, writing on Instagram: 'trying to process this but alas i shan't CANT WAIT TO JOIN THE ERAS TOUR IN LATIN AMERICA thank u @taylorswift u the 1 :') this is a dream come true'. [46]

When she made her Eras tour debut in Mexico City, Sabrina opened by projecting her first-ever YouTube video on to a huge screen. It showed her, aged nine, singing Swift's 'Picture to Burn'. She later told *Vanity Fair*: 'It is magnificent to grow up idolising someone, and then meet them, and they are all the things that you hoped that they would be.' [47]

It was a dizzying moment for the young star, and she loved every second. '[Taylor's] stadiums make my shows look like clubs,' she told *Vogue*. '[I loved] watching her keep their attention as if she's playing in their living room.' [48]

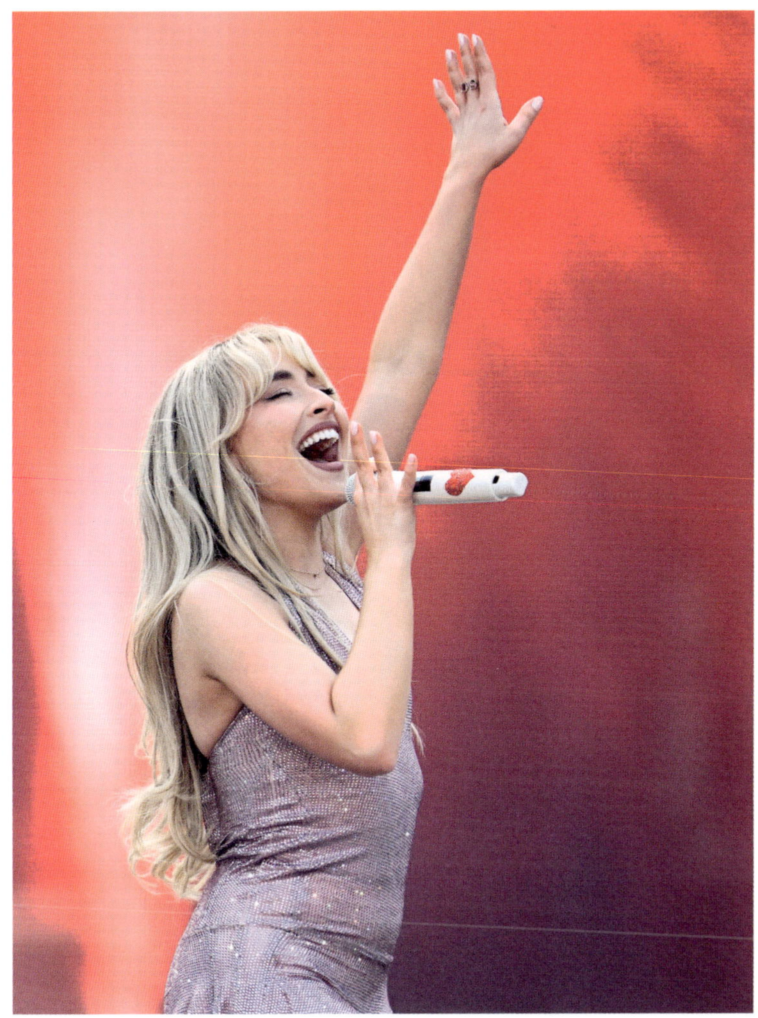

INTRODUCING THE OUTRO

Thanks to her own tour and her Eras shows, Sabrina was starting to get a lot of attention – and it certainly helped that her 'Nonsense' outros started to go viral on TikTok. Sabrina had started writing a new outro for every live show, tailoring it to the city in which she was performing, and it soon became an iconic moment of each set. Fans started listening out for the cheeky new rhymes, and entire websites were set up dedicated to documenting every outro.

Here are just a few:

Buenos Aires: 'When I'm in the bedroom looking sexy / He's having a ball, he call me "Messi" / Argentina, will you be my bestie?'

Rio de Janeiro: 'Sipping on me like a caipirinha / How to turn me on, boy, I can teach ya / My new name is Ipanema Brina.'

Sydney: 'Yeah, he's pretty cute but will our kids be? / This country's so big, I hope it fit me / I Vegemite be in love with you, Sydney.'

Sabrina told the *Guardian*: 'I've written literally 900 outros. I've said a lot of provocative things that I don't do or feel. I need [more] rhymes, I'm running low!'[49] The outros gave her a chance to share her cheeky, playful side with fans – and they loved it.

'I think they taught me a little more wordplay and a couple more innuendos. That might have bled into the next album.'[50]

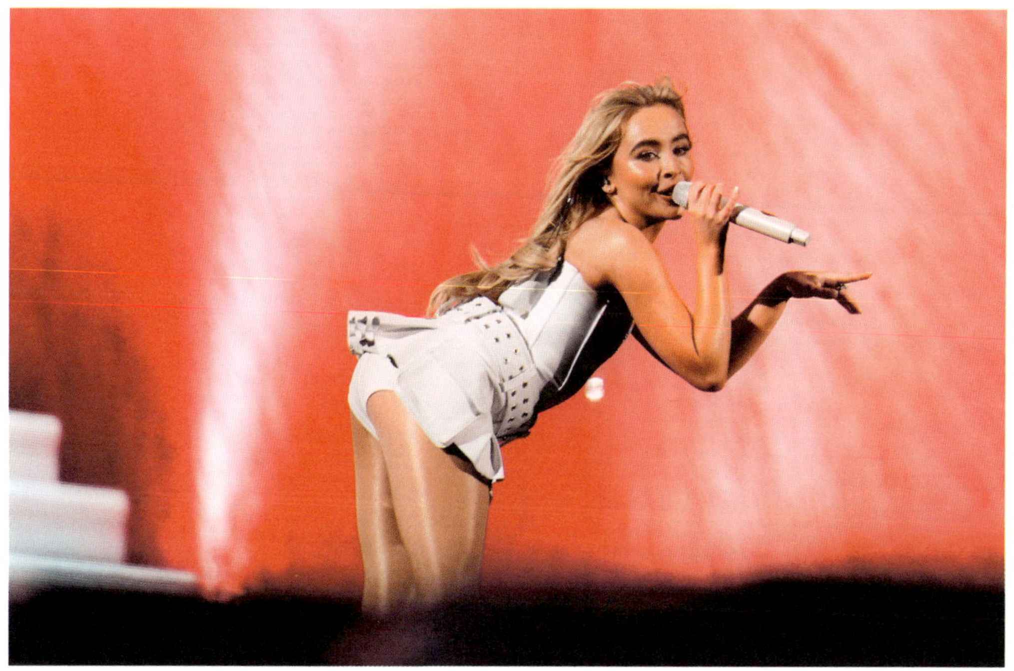

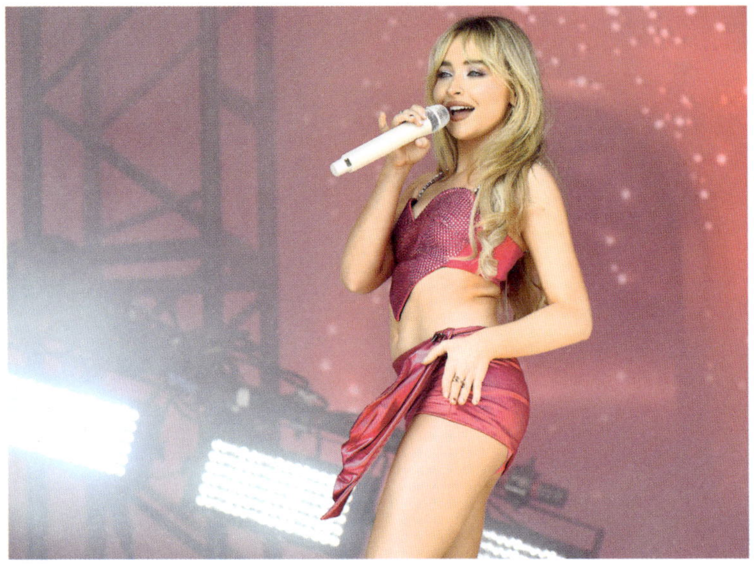

FEATHER

To celebrate Halloween, Sabrina released the horror-themed music video for her single 'Feather' on 31 October 2023. The video depicts men disrespecting her before dying horribly, ending with her emerging from a baby-pink hearse and dancing around in a church in front of their pastel-coloured coffins.

Controversially, the location for the video shoot was an active Catholic church. The priest who gave permission for filming was 'stripped of his administrative duties',[51] with a Mass of Reparation held soon afterwards.

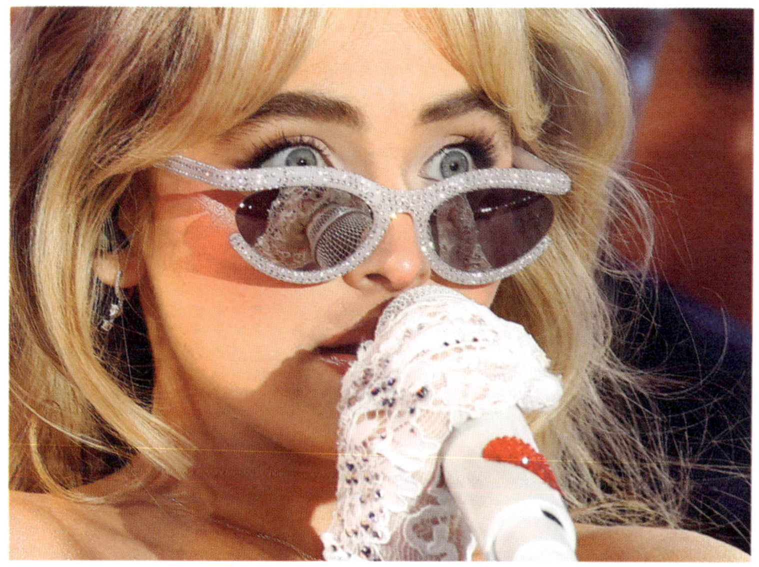

ENDING THE YEAR STRONG

What with the success of her album and live shows, 2023 was a big year for Sabrina. She marked the final days of the year with a series of extra wins, releasing a festive version of her hit 'Nonsense', being named *Variety*'s Rising Star of 2023 and performing as part of *Dick Clark's New Year's Rockin' Eve* in Times Square. Sabrina wore a white corseted minidress, fluffy white wrap and elbow-length lace gloves and sang 'Feather' followed by 'Nonsense'. In true Sabrina style, she gave the outro its own NYE spin: 'Clark is everybody's favourite dick type / Make a toast to everyone you dislike / Balls are dropping everywhere at midnight'.[52]

ESPRESSO TIME

*The Sabrina success train gathers
speed – and it seems unstoppable.*

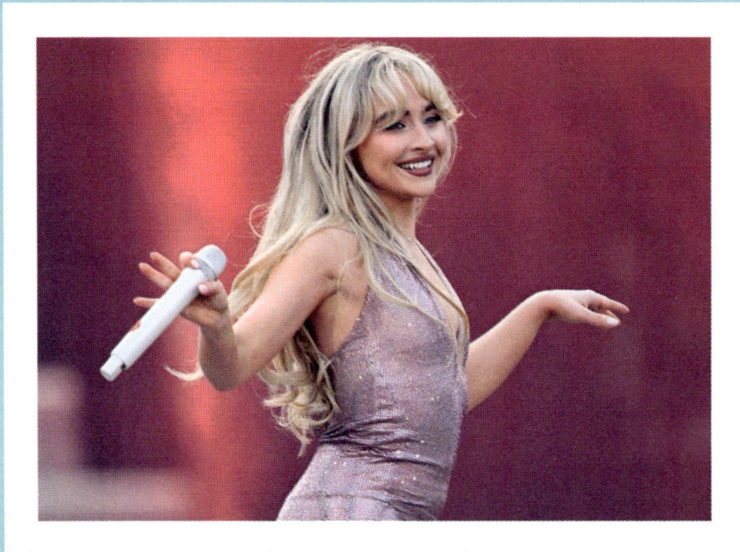

'I JUST LOVE THAT
PEOPLE GET MY SENSE
OF HUMOUR.'[53]

THE WEATHER CAN'T STOP TAYBRINA

As 2024 began, the Taybrina era continued, with Sabrina supporting Taylor Swift for the Australia and Singapore stretch of the Eras tour.

For one show in Sydney, huge thunderstorms caused chaos, and Sabrina's set had to be cancelled while the stadium's 81,000-strong crowd was evacuated due to the weather. However, once the tempest had calmed, Taylor took to the stage as scheduled – and brought out Sabrina for a surprise duet. The pair sang 'White Horse' and 'Coney Island', delighting the crowd. Sabrina later wrote on Instagram: '9 year old Sabrina singing white horse would never see this shit coming. i love you so so so dearly taylor. always have always will.'[54]

'I was just so mindblown by the crowds that would sing along to all these songs.'[55]

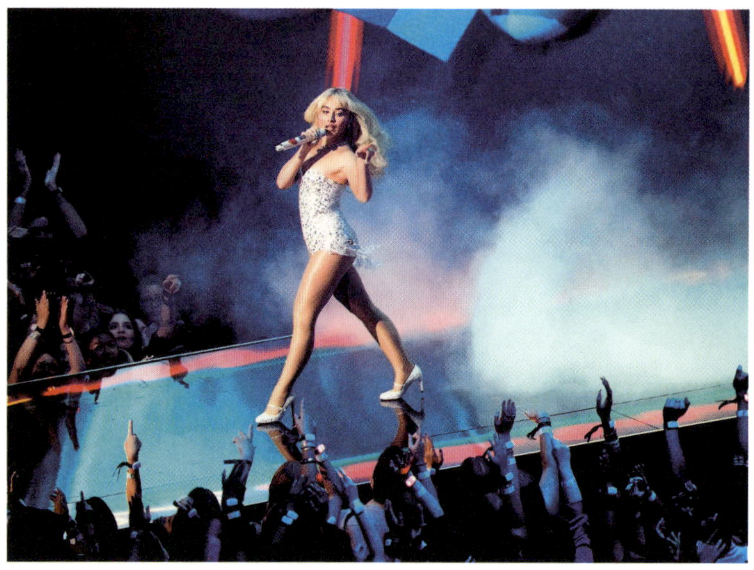

ESPRESSO, EXTRA HOT

On 11 April 2024, Sabrina's single 'Espresso' was released – and the lives of baristas the world over changed forever. With its irresistible beat and endlessly quotable lyrics, 'Espresso' was always going to be *the* hit of summer 2024, but the music video catapulted it to a whole new level. She told *W Magazine* about the inspiration for the video: 'To me, "Espresso" sounded like when you turn on a vintage radio at the beach. And I did want to make it a little bit ridiculous, because that's up my alley.'[56]

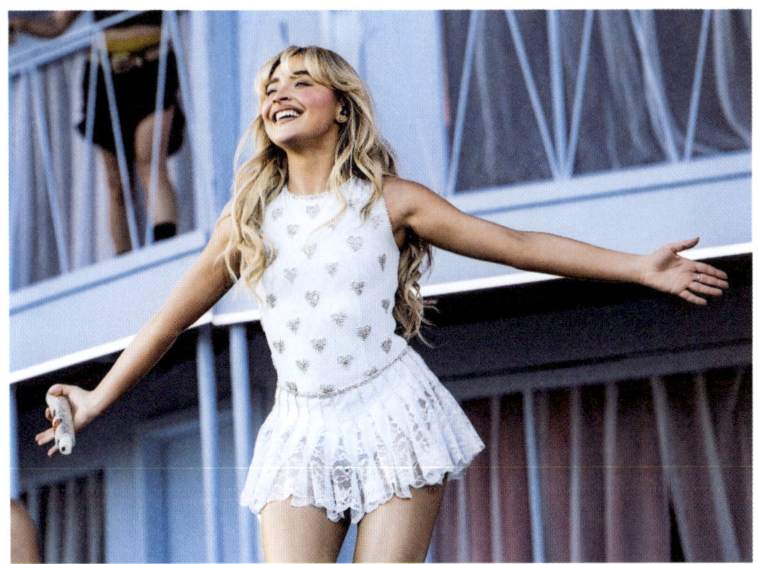

COACHELLA'S CAFFEINE HIT

Sabrina debuted 'Espresso' at the legendary festival Coachella. Her set opened with a clip from a fake 1950s-style film noir titled *The Wreckage*. The entire set went down a storm, but the crowd's reaction to 'Espresso' showed that her instincts had been exactly right: this song was special.

'I was writing all these sad songs and "Espresso" was like the one breath of fresh air. In the midst of it all, I was like … this is still such a huge part of me – this mentality and the sense of humour and playfulness.' [57]

SABRINA NIGHT LIVE

20 May 2024 saw Sabrina make her first-ever appearance on the iconic US TV show *Saturday Night Live*. She was introduced by Jake Gyllenhaal, and performed 'Espresso' in a red babydoll dress while dancing around a stage set up to resemble a cocktail bar.

She later told *Time* magazine that it was a real dream come true: 'There were so many things I dreamt of doing as a little girl that I got to do this year that felt like such a cool, sweet little bucket-list moment for my younger self. I literally threw up when I found out about *SNL*. Not to be graphic.'[58]

Sabrina's association with *SNL* wouldn't end there, though. As we'll see on page 95 she later became a key part of one of the show's most popular skits.

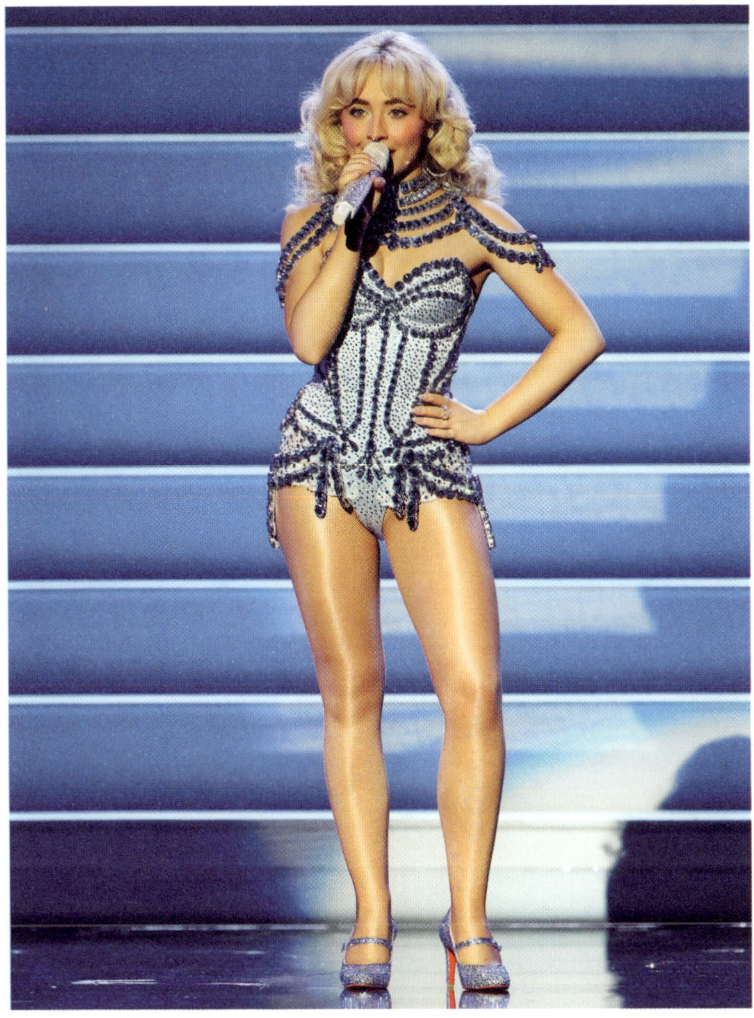

EVEN THE BBC CAN'T TELL SABRINA WHAT TO DO

Back in 2023, Sabrina scandalised the BBC with a particularly cheeky 'Nonsense' outro when she played a *Live Lounge* session. For her appearance at Radio 1's Big Weekend in May 2024, bosses apparently asked her to tone it down a bit. Her response, delivered in a butter-wouldn't-melt voice but with a playful glint in her eye, was to perform the following outro live onstage, complete with hand gestures: 'BBC told me to keep it PG / BBC I wish I had it in me / There's a double meaning if you dig deep.'

In an interview with the *Guardian*, Sabrina later said: '"Nonsense" happened like a storm in my life, so I didn't really have time to consider one too many dick jokes.'[59]

It may have had execs hot under the collar, but UK band Coldplay are clearly Sabrina stans, inviting the diminutive songstress to join them onstage for 'Magic' during their set at the Big Weekend. Frontman Chris Martin even changed the lyrics to their hit 'Fix You' to include some of the words to 'Espresso'. She sure made an impression.

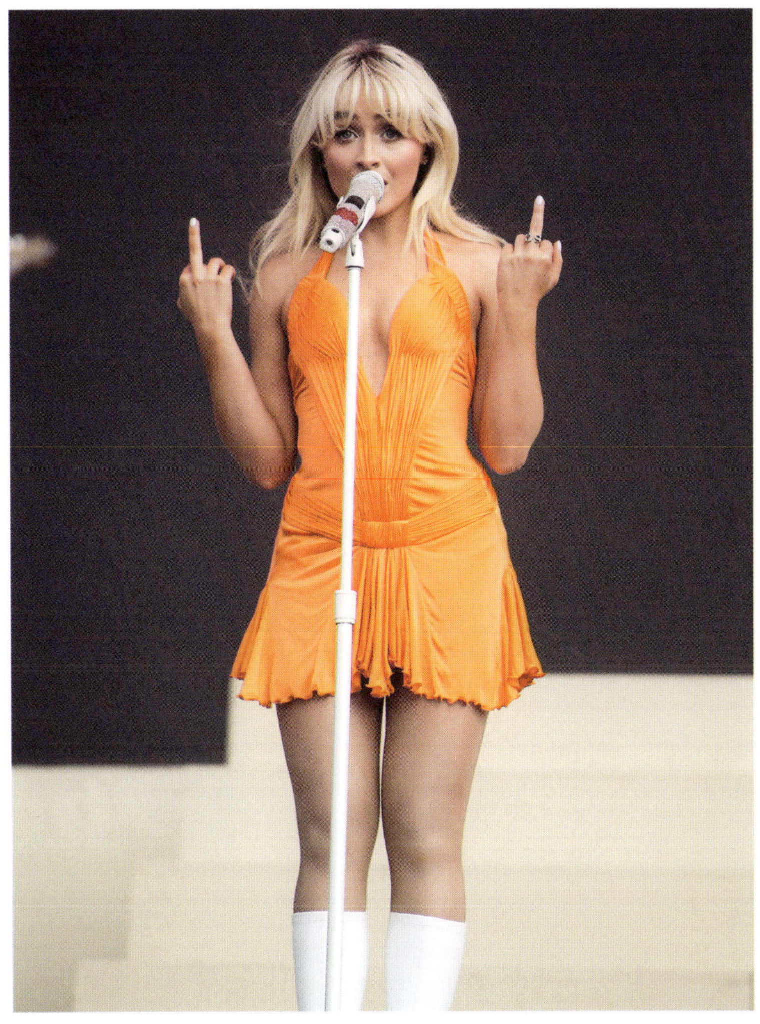

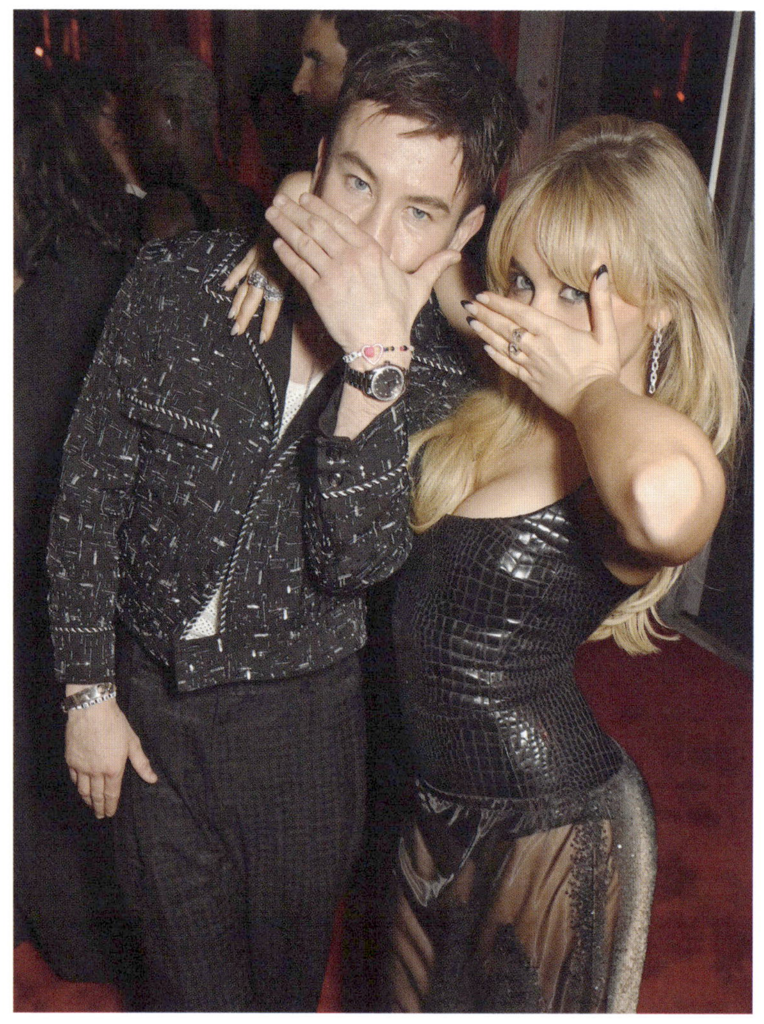

PLEASE PLEASE PLEASE

The hits just kept coming: next up was 'Please Please Please', which was released on 6 June 2024. The single was accompanied by a video featuring *Saltburn* star Barry Keoghan, whom Sabrina was dating at the time, although they have since gone their separate ways. When asked if the song was about him, Sabrina was evasive: 'Obviously, I write songs about exactly how I feel, so I guess I can't be surprised that people are interested in who and what those songs are about. That's something that comes with the territory.'[60]

The video picks up where 'Espresso' left off, with Sabrina getting bailed out after her arrest and falling for a man who has also been arrested, then watching with growing frustration as he fails to mend his ways. It ends with her handcuffing him to a chair and planting a lipsticked kiss on his taped-up mouth – perhaps a not-so-subtle warning to anyone thinking of *dis*pleasing her.

'Please Please Please' marked Sabrina's first number one on the Billboard Hot 100.

I'm so blunt and forward. I feel like, what is the reason that we're all hiding from each other when these are just real things. Sometimes men embarrass you. That's just normal.'[61]

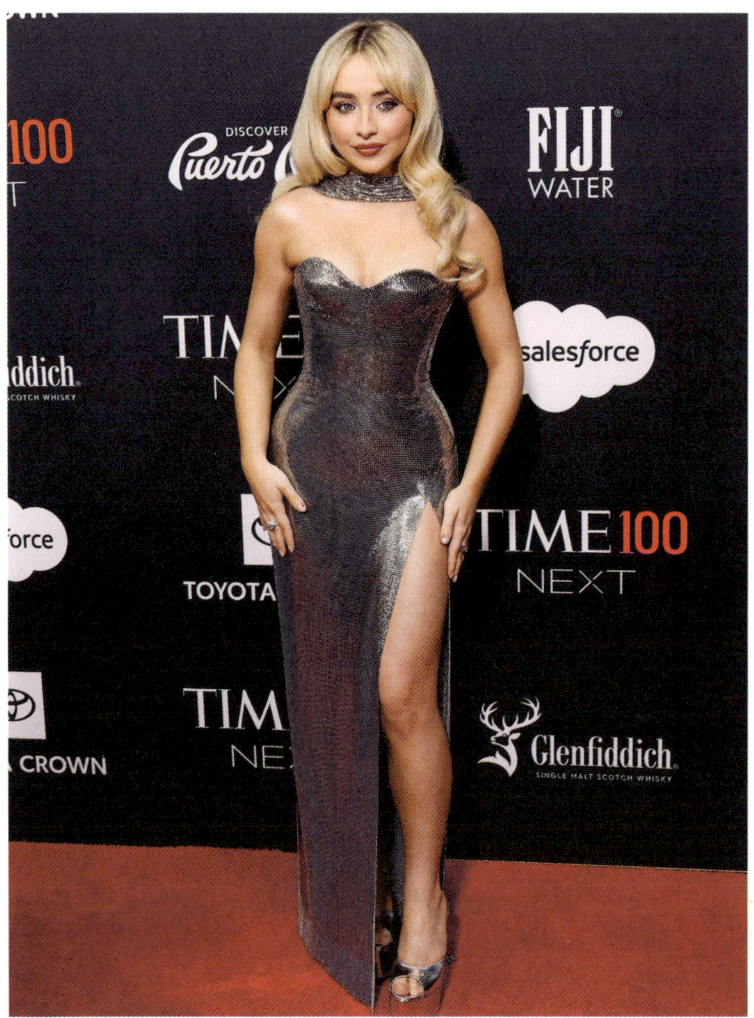

PLEASING THE GOV BALL

The weekend of 7–9 June 2024 saw New Yorkers descend on the iconic Governors Ball music festival, where Sabrina treated them to an exhilarating live set. She sparkled in a glittering pale yellow minidress adorned with rhinestones and featuring a heart-shaped cut-out at the chest, which she paired with a bedazzled pair of platforms.

During the set, she spotted a fan in the crowd holding up a sign that said 'Please, please, please play "Please Please Please"'. She laughed and said, 'Look, I know I said I can't relate to desperation, but – I'm just a girl. So … could you please, please, please help me sing this song?'[62]

The audience were only too happy to oblige. Even though the song had come out just a day or two before, they sang along with every word.

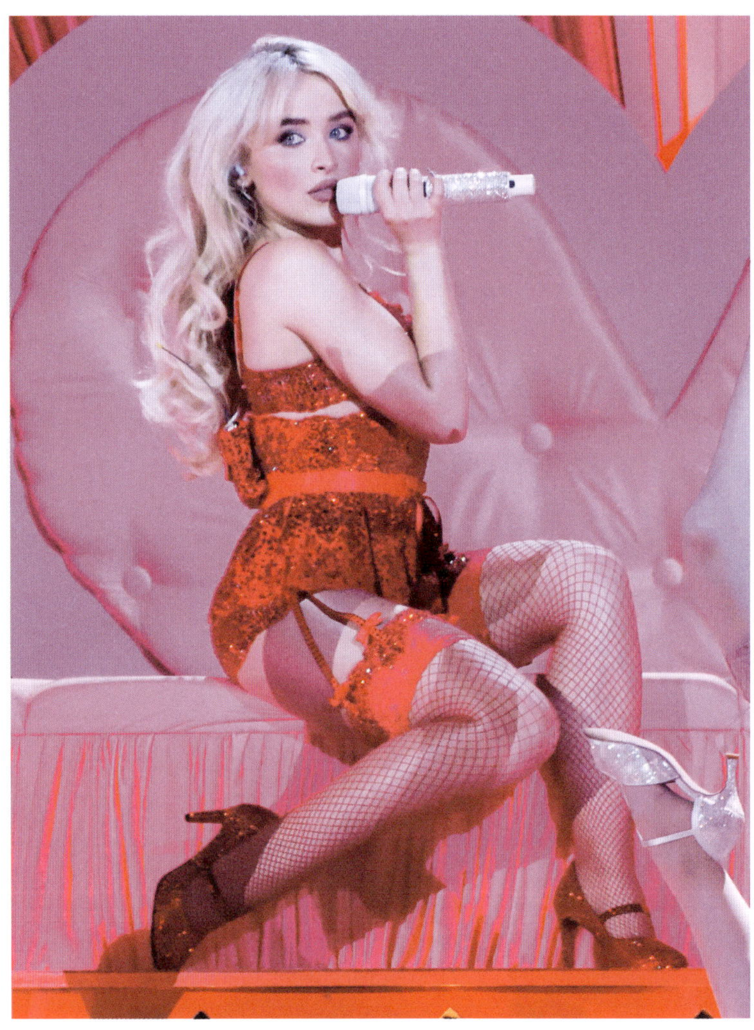

SHORT N' SPICY

In July 2024, Sabrina braved *Hot Ones*, the popular online show where celebrities eat increasingly spicy chicken wings while being interviewed, and delighted fans with her playful reaction to the extreme spice. As she sampled sauces that crept their way up the Scoville scale (the final one registered a tongue-smoking 2,693,000 Scoville heat units), she made some classically Sabrina-esque remarks, including:

'My palate is being opened [...] My senses are starting to bubble.'[63]

'Has anyone ever projectiled in front of you?'

'Has anyone ever *sued* you?!'

'I really like incorporating covers, because I started out covering— This one is *really* spicy, Sean. It's like my tongue [is] trying to revert back into my throat.'

'That answer was bullshit, like, I don't know what I just told you. I don't know how I'm feeling right now. What did I just say?'

'[My album] is called *Short n' Sweet*. Notice I didn't call it Short n' Spicy, because I like sweet things better.'

SPARKS FLY

On 10 August 2024, Sabrina headlined the Outside Lands festival, playing to a huge crowd. During the set, she invited singer Kacey Musgraves onstage and the pair performed Nancy Sinatra's 'These Boots Are Made For Walkin''. Sabrina then treated the crowd to hit after hit. At the end of 'Nonsense', one of her backing dancers, dressed in a smart suit, presented her with a scroll, from which she read her outro, including the line 'Outside Lands, it's like thou art inside me'.

The show was so electrifying that, at the end of her final song, 'Espresso', some of the onstage pyrotechnics appeared to malfunction, showering Carpenter in sparks and causing her to run away screaming. Luckily, although her performance was on fire, the popstar was unharmed.

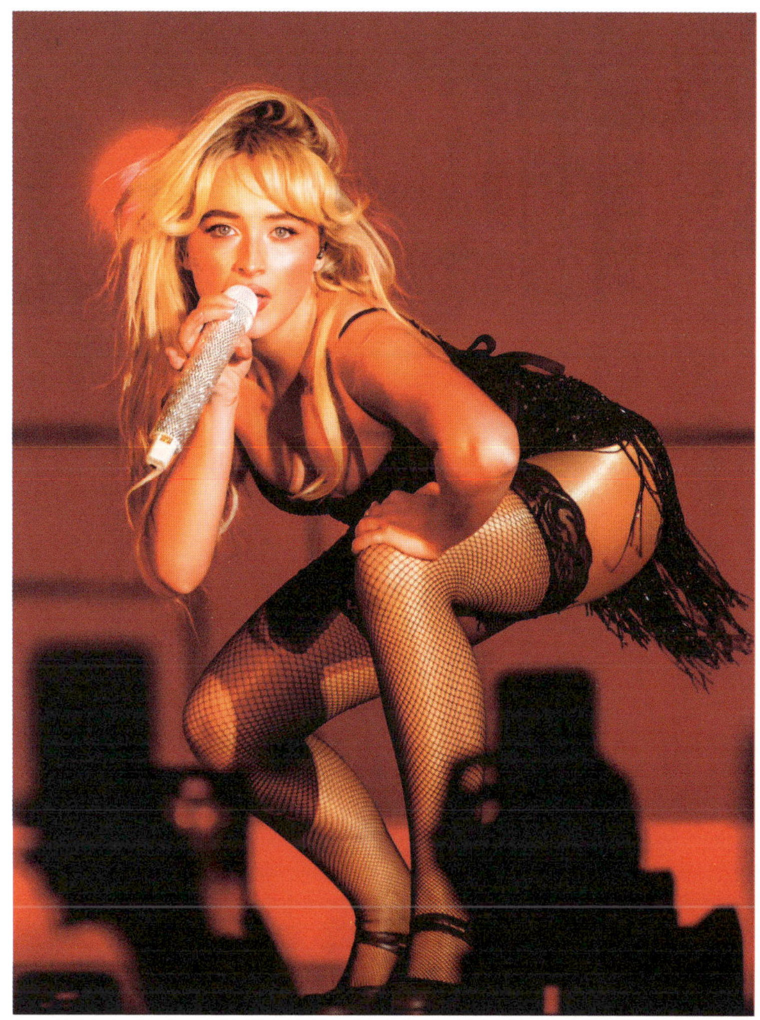

THE TONIGHT SHOW STARRING SABRINA CARPENTER

On 22 August 2024, Sabrina appeared on *The Tonight Show Starring Jimmy Fallon* to mark the release of *Short n' Sweet*, which came out the following day. During their interview, Jimmy revealed that 'Espresso' was now certified platinum, and was one of the fastest songs to ever hit one billion streams on Spotify. He also shared with the audience that 'Please Please Please' had hit no.1 on the Spotify chart – knocking off 'Espresso' – and that Sabrina was the first artist since the Beatles to have two songs at once debut within the top 3 on the Billboard Hot 100. She didn't believe him, noting: 'That one sounds fake to me.'[64]

Perhaps one of the best moments of their interview came when Jimmy shared a video a fan had filmed at an Adele show, which showed the legendary British singer explaining that she sings 'Espresso' to herself late at night: 'I got into bed last night [and it was] a very late night for me, I'm normally in bed by like 9pm. [And] I found myself singing: "I'm working late, cause I'm a singerrrr" – that song is my jam.'[65]

'Honestly, it does really feel like a self-titled album for me – also cause Short n' Sweet is sort of like Sabrina in another language to me. [And it's …] very much blunt, very forward, very fun.' [66]

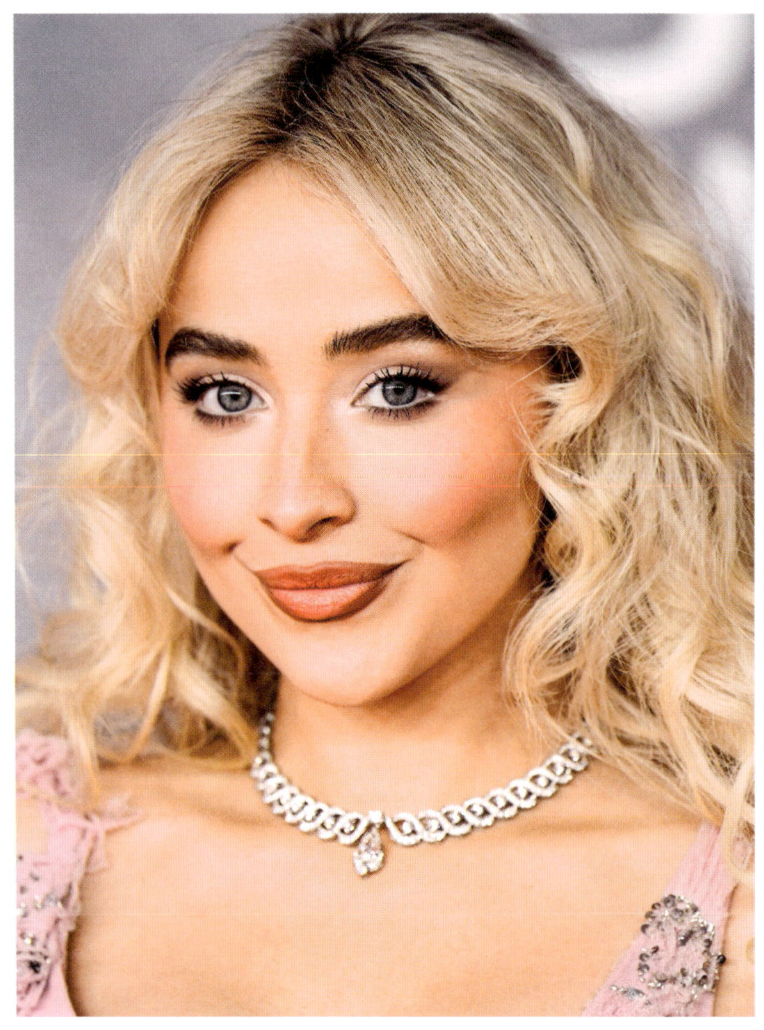

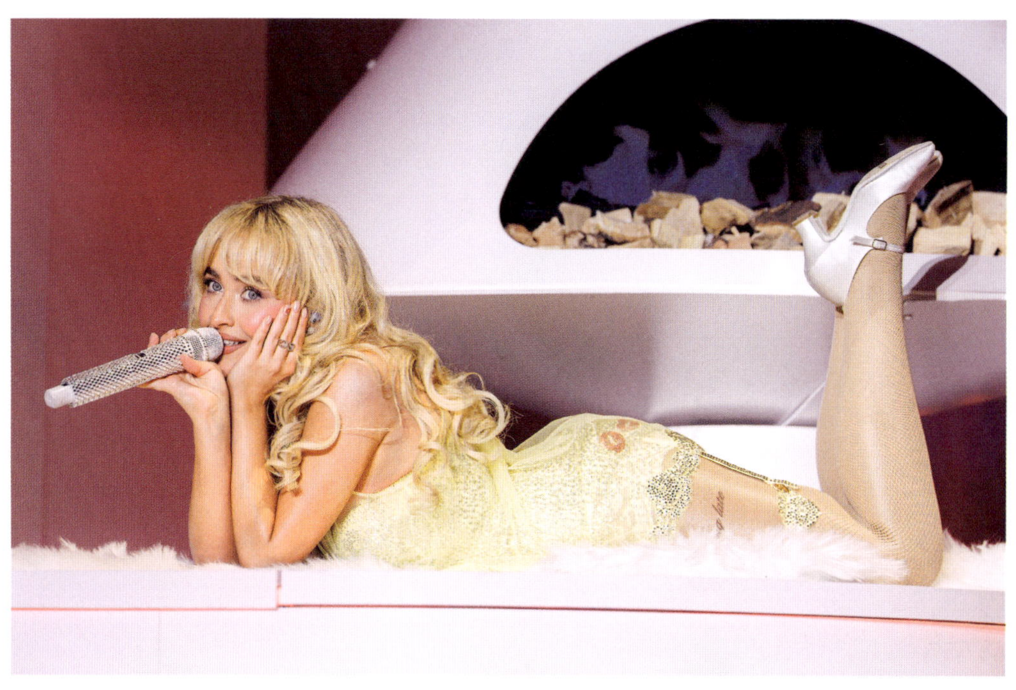

HOT DATE

In August 2024, Sabrina appeared in the cult-hit web series *Chicken Shop Date* with Amelia Dimoldenberg. At the start of the interview, Sabrina pretended to think she was on *Hot Ones* (see page 67). Her dry humour was a perfect match for Amelia's deadpan oddities, and the pair vibed in what can only be described as a gloriously awkward way. When Amelia asked her how she was enjoying London, Sabrina responded: 'Someone called me a wanker; I feel like I've really lived the London experience.'[67]

She also announced, very seriously: 'People think I'm really short, but I'm actually super tall.'

When Amelia asked if she'd rather date a barista or a barrister, Sabrina replied: 'I think baristas flirt too much.' Maybe with you, Sabrina.

SHORT AND SASSY

As her success continues, Sabrina shares her cheeky sense of humour with the world.

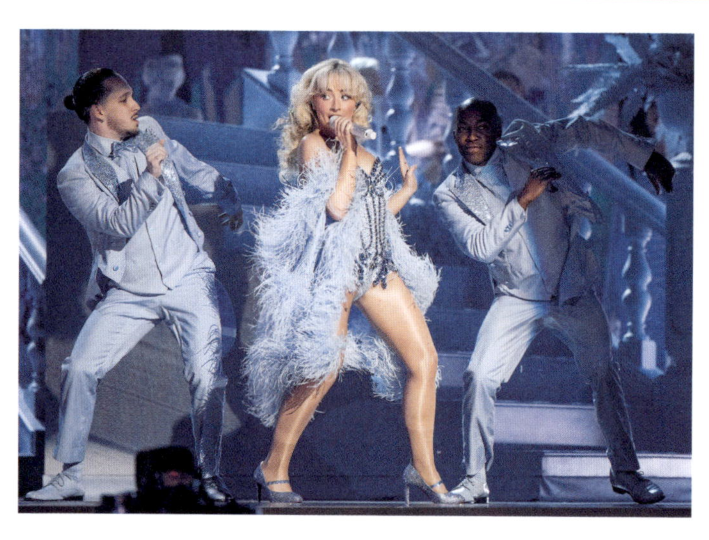

'IT'LL PROBABLY BITE ME
IN THE ASS AT SOME POINT,
BUT [*SHORT N' SWEET* HAS]
BEEN A REALLY THERAPEUTIC
ALBUM – TO BE ABLE TO JUST
SAY WHAT I'M THINKING'[68]

GOOD TASTE

On 23 August 2024, Sabrina released the third single from *Short n' Sweet*, 'Taste'. The song was accompanied by an impossibly glamorous – and gory – video starring Sabrina and *Wednesday* actress Jenna Ortega. The video's opening echoes the ending of the 'Please Please Please' video, as Sabrina peruses a bed laid out with weapons, handcuffs and a teddy bear whose mouth is covered with kiss-marked tape.

The video was inspired by cult-classic film *Death Becomes Her*, and shows Sabrina and her love rival Jenna trying to murder each other in increasingly violent ways as they fight over a boy.

Just before the video's release, Sabrina told Jimmy Fallon: 'Honestly, I think it's my favourite [video] I've ever done.'[69]

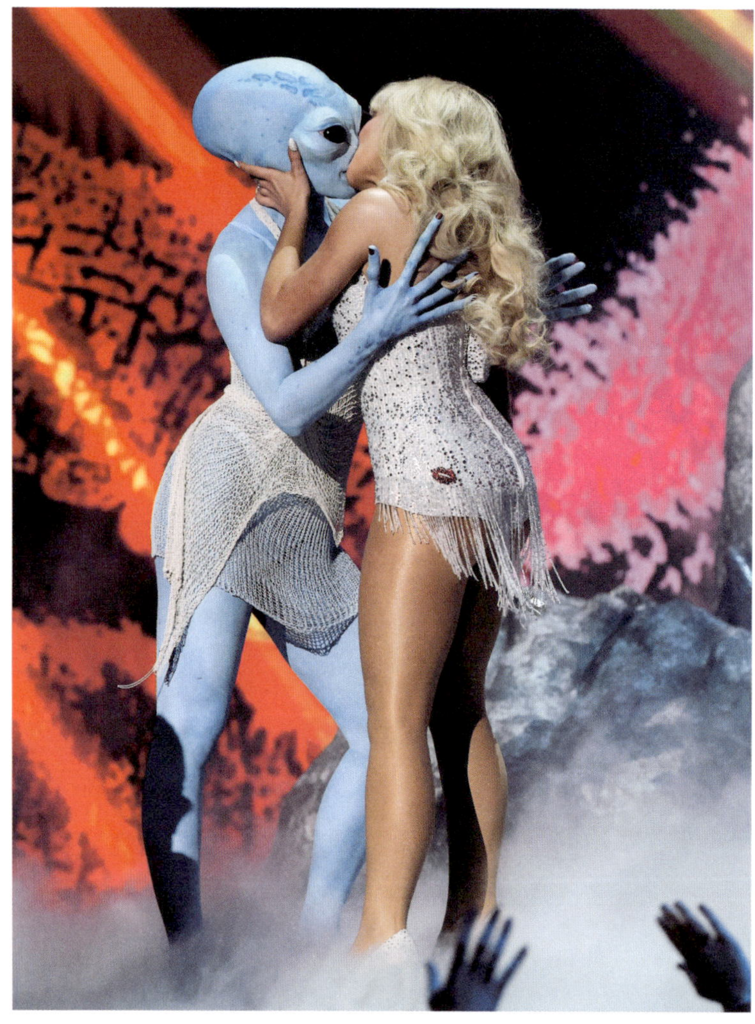

OUT OF THIS WORLD

'I grew up watching those performances and being like, I want to do that.' [70]

On 11 September 2024, the annual MTV Video Music Awards (VMAs) were held. Sabrina received seven nominations, and dazzled on the red carpet in a vintage-inspired silver gown by Bob Mackie – which was previously worn by Madonna back in 1991.

She won Song of the Year for 'Espresso' – no surprises there – and made a gracious acceptance speech that was frequently interrupted by rapturous applause, causing her to quip: 'If you clap after everything I say, they're gonna call me off the stage.' [71]

The crowd was also treated to a performance of a medley of her hits 'Please Please Please', 'Taste' and 'Espresso'. The set opened with Sabrina sitting on a silver swing high above the audience, before descending into a lunar landscape inspired by the VMAs' iconic Moon Person trophy, complete with astronauts and an alien. She had another Madonna-callback moment when she kissed the alien during her set, perhaps echoing the kisses the Material Girl famously shared with Britney Spears and Christina Aguilera while performing at the VMAs back in 2003.

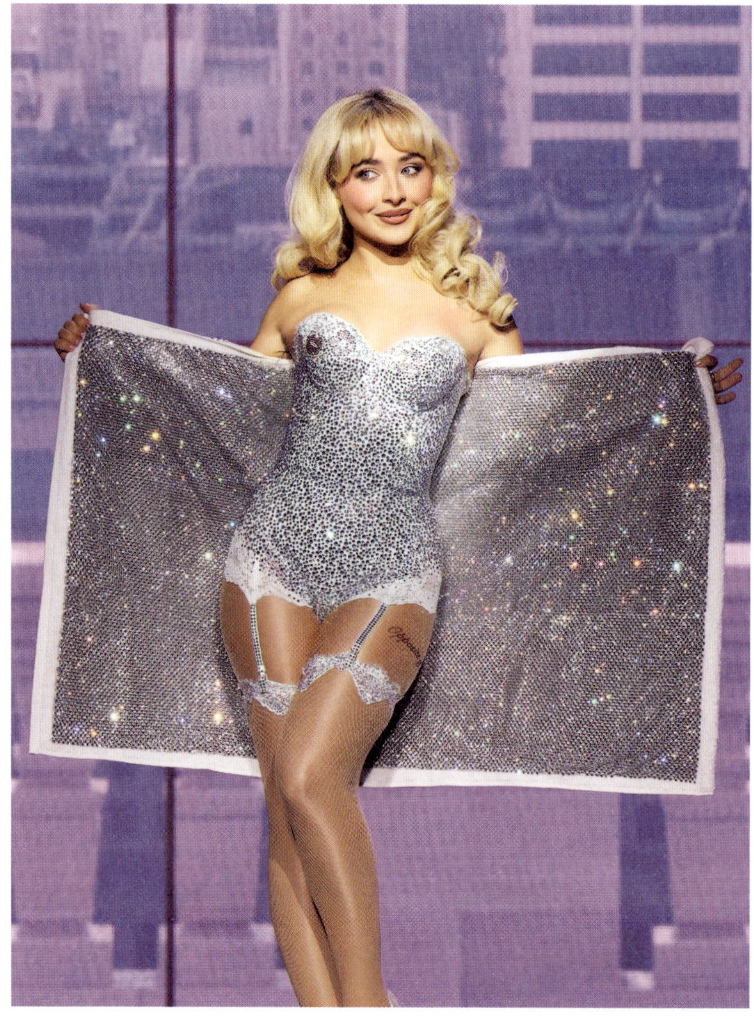

SHORT N' SWEET (N' SILLY)

In September 2024, Sabrina embarked on the *Short n' Sweet* tour, which opened in Columbus, USA, and, at the time of writing, is scheduled to continue until November 2025, with shows in the US, Canada, Ireland, UK and mainland Europe.

Videos of the start of the concert quickly went viral online. The show opens with Sabrina in a bubble bath, suddenly realising she's late and rushing out onto the stage wrapped in her towel. As the fans scream with delight, she gives a cheeky smile and removes the towel, revealing one of her iconic outfits. Another beloved moment from the show features her pretending she's too short to reach the mic.

The tour allows Sabrina to showcase her playful sense of humour, and celebrates the way she manages to find the comedy in almost anything. In an interview with Zane Lowe, she mused: 'When you're at the point in your life when you're, like, almost at your wit's end, everything is funny. Everything can be funny because it's all stupid.'[72]

'It's my first-ever arena tour […] and I'm so small and the stages are so big.'[73]

THE GREATEST SHOWGIRL

As the tour continued, Sabrina won widespread praise for the quality and pizzazz of her stage shows. She told *Vogue*: 'Growing up, those were the kinds of shows I would want to go to. Ones where I thought I knew what I was getting, but I got something completely different.'[74]

To keep her fans on the edge of their seats, she enjoyed mixing things up, spinning a bottle onstage to choose different cover songs (highlights so far have included '9 to 5' by Dolly Parton and 'Mamma Mia' by ABBA) and interacting with audience members.

In an interview with *Vogue*, she said: '*Short n' Sweet* is absolutely me. There's no, like, alter ego. But it's definitely a more emphasised version of me. It's interesting because I'm able to dress in this way where you would kind of expect to hear a voice from the 60s. But then when I'm speaking to the audience, I'm just myself.'[75]

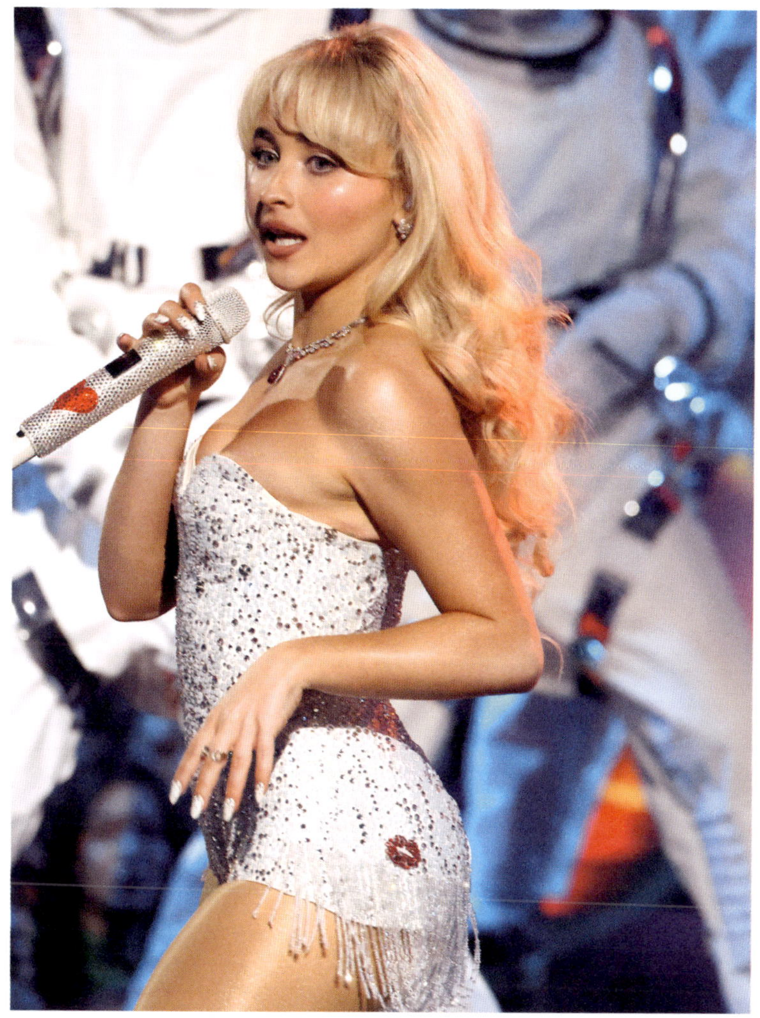

HAVE YOU EVER TRIED ...?

For the *Short n' Sweet* tour, Sabrina made the decision to retire her adored 'Nonsense' outros (see page 48). As she explained to *Time* magazine: 'Maybe I'll feel random one day and bring [the outros] back. [But] that was that album, that era. You've got to keep a thing good.'[76]

Fans had no need to be disappointed, however, as Sabrina brought a new playful element to her live shows, in the form of the 'Juno' positions. While singing 'Juno', she approaches the front of the stage, fixes the audience with a cheeky gaze, and asks: 'Have you ever tried this one?', before demonstrating a *Kama Sutra*-worthy pose.

She told *Vogue*: 'Well, initially I thought I'd just rotate between a couple, but I have this relationship with my fans where I know they want more from me. I don't want to let them down. So sometimes I go: *Oh, you know what? Fuck it. It's Thursday. Let me give them a new one.*'[77]

The cheeky new addition to the show might make some people wonder how it feels for Sabrina when family members are in the audience, but it's not a concern: 'My fans online are like, I can't believe she's bending over in front of her grandparents! And I'm like, girl, they are not paying attention to that. They're just like, I can't believe all these people are here.'[78]

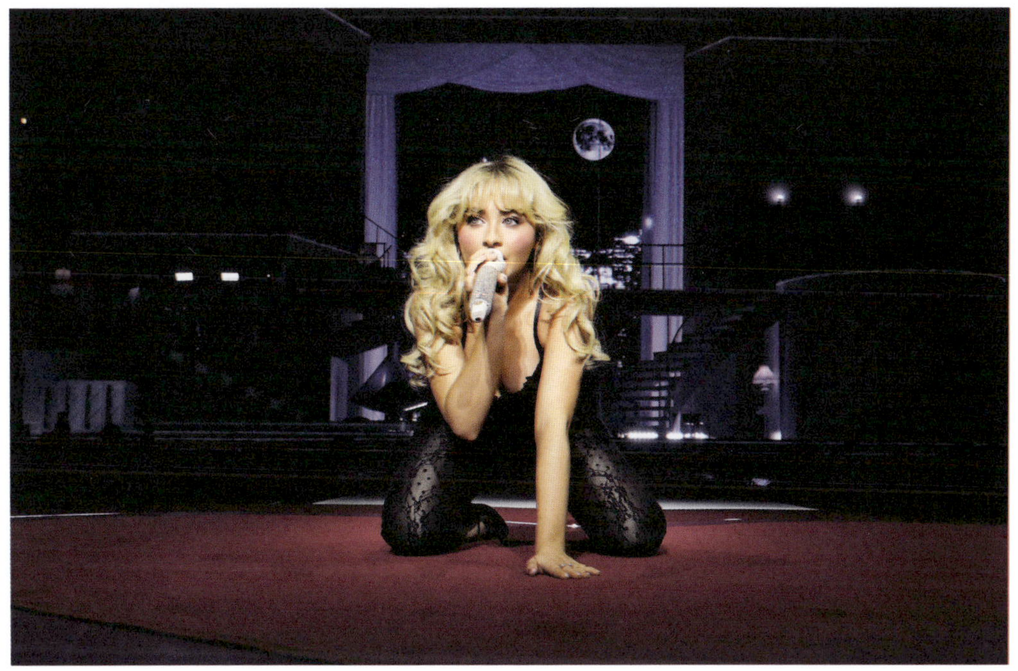

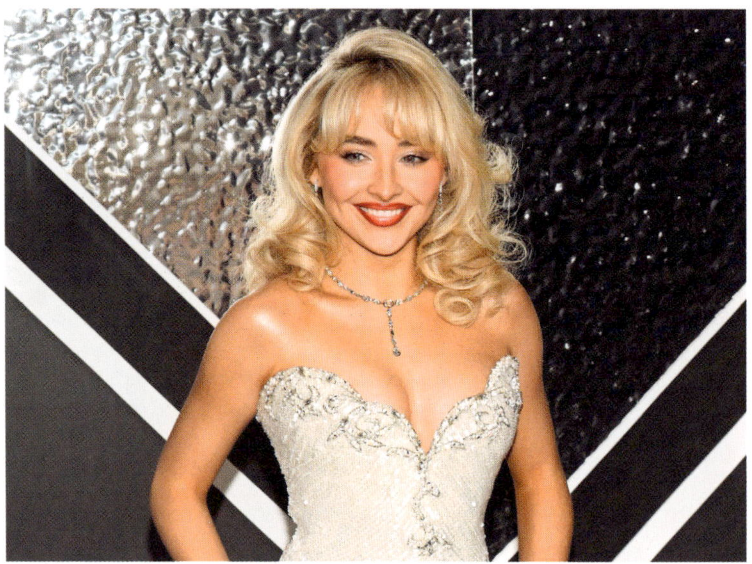

BED CHEM

On 8 October 2024, Sabrina released a new single: 'Bed Chem', a steamy, synthy tune with breathy vocals. It was accompanied by a lyric video showing Sabrina sitting in a lush garden wearing a pale green babydoll dress.

During her NPR Tiny Desk concert (see page 97), she explained the inspiration behind the song, saying: 'Some people know me for … I guess being explicitly horny. It's not as simple as that.' She revealed that the idea for the song actually came from a sleepover with her best friend, Paloma.

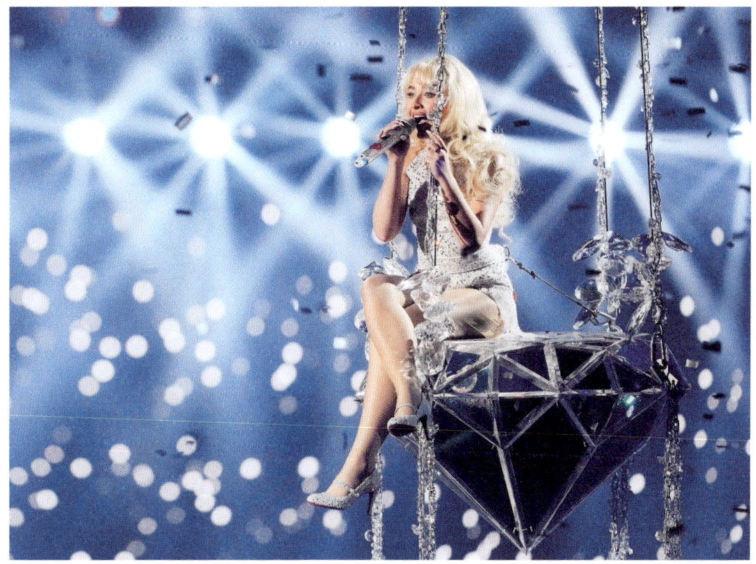

STRANGER SINGS

During her *Short n' Sweet* tour, Sabrina has taken to 'arresting' a member of the audience every night, presenting them with a pair of pink fluffy handcuffs. On 22 October 2024 in Atlanta, Georgia, *Stranger Things* star Millie Bobby Brown had taken a break from filming to attend. Sabrina appeared to spot Millie in the crowd, saying, 'This girl is so hot ... I've never fallen in love at a concert before, but stranger things have happened... we have to arrest you because you're so beautiful.' Millie held out her hands and said, 'Please arrest me!', causing Sabrina to hand her a pair of those iconic fluffy handcuffs. The footage of their playful interaction went viral.

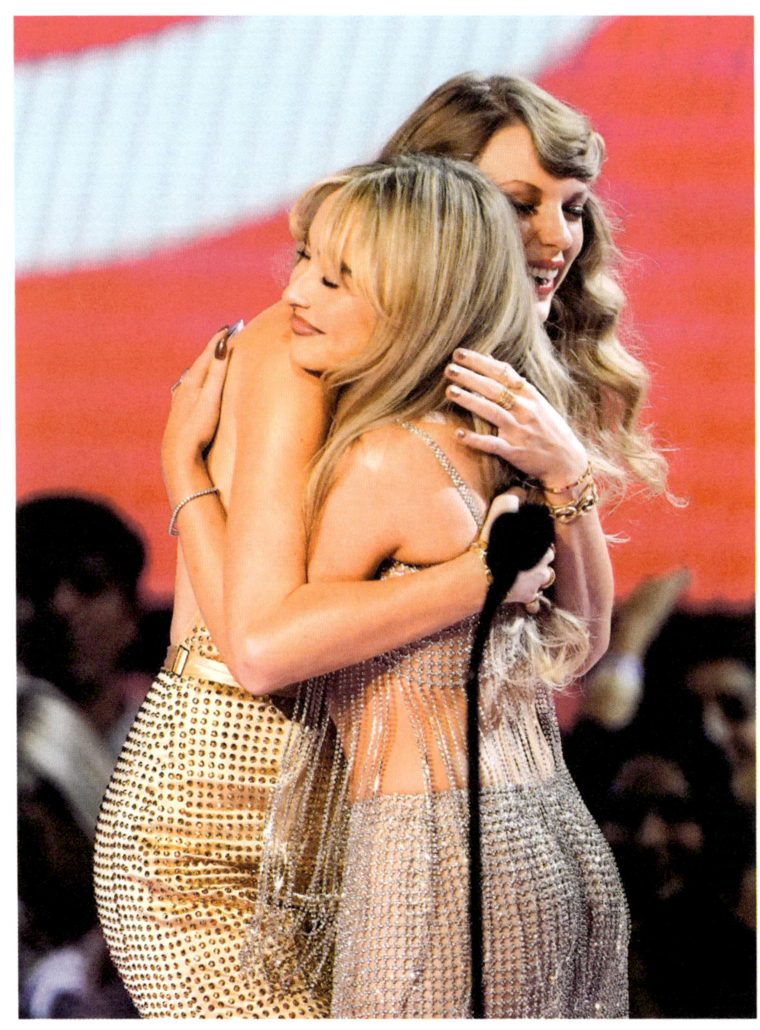

THE POP PRINCESS OF OUR DREAMS

On 26 October 2024, Sabrina was taking a much-needed night off from her hectic touring schedule – at least, we thought she was. Her friend Taylor Swift was performing in New Orleans that night, and at one point during the show got her guitar out and said she wanted to sing a cover, because 'it's been stuck in my head, and it would make me feel good if I knew 65,000 other people had it stuck in their heads, just like I do'.[79]

As she began to play 'Espresso', the crowd went wild – but not as wild as they went a few moments later, when Taylor phoned Sabrina and, over speakerphone, invited her to come and join her onstage. Within seconds, Sabrina was there, and the two performed a mash-up of 'Espresso', 'Please Please Please' and Taylor's 'Is it Over Now?'.

In an Instagram post a few days later, Taylor wrote: 'One of the things I'll always remember from this weekend was getting to surprise the crowd with a performance by the pop princess of our dreams: @sabrinacarpenter.'[80]

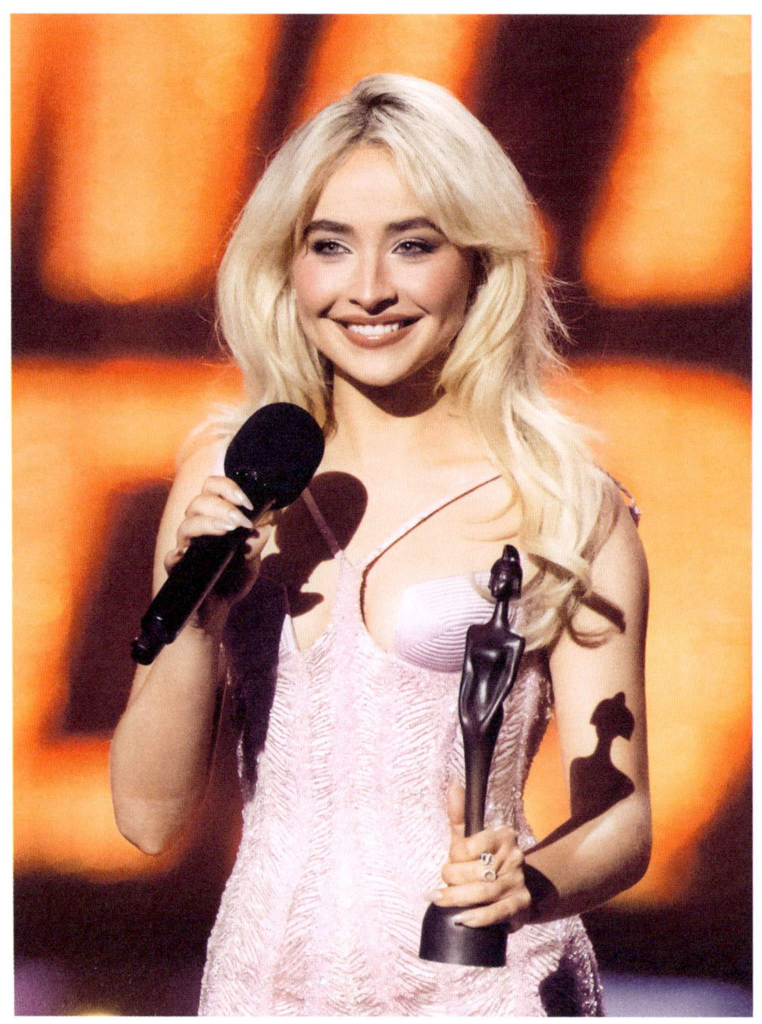

SPOOKILY DEVOTED

As we saw on page 50, Sabrina loves Halloween – and on 30 October 2024, she dressed up for the occasion during the Dallas, Texas, stop of her Short n' Sweet tour. She treated the audience to several different outfits, including a glittery green Tinkerbell dress with wings and a Playboy bunny-style get-up, but the highlight came when she donned a tight black catsuit in the style of Olivia Newton John's character Sandy from *Grease*, and gave a stunning rendition of 'Hopelessly Devoted to You'. The crowd sang along with enthusiasm, relishing the sight of one blonde bombshell honouring another.

Sharing some photos of the incredible outfit on her Instagram, Sabrina wrote: 'a short n' spooky halloween'.[81]

JUST GETTING STARTED

As her star continues to rise, it looks like there is nothing Sabrina can't do.

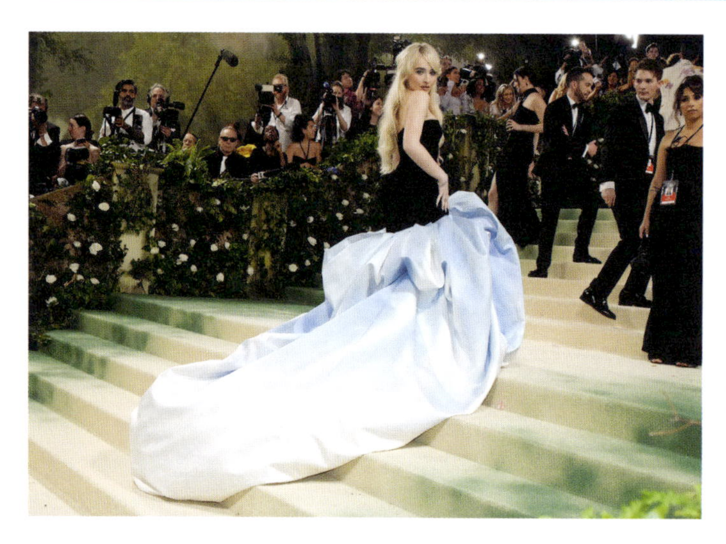

'[CHART SUCCESS IS] NOT THE REASON I WRITE MUSIC AND IT'S NOT THE REASON I'LL EVER WRITE MUSIC. IT'S LIKE THE SPRINKLES ON TOP OF THE SUNDAE.'[82]

DIRECT FROM DOMINGO!

As we saw on page 58, Sabrina is a big fan of *Saturday Night Live* – but it turns out the *SNL* team are also big fans of hers. October 2024 saw the creation of a skit that quickly became a fan favourite. It featured a set of bridesmaids (including Ariana Grande) singing a painfully off-key parody of 'Espresso' instead of making a speech at their friend Kelsey's wedding. During the song, they revealed that Kelsey had met a very handsome man named Domingo during her bachelorette vacation. The characters reappeared in a later episode singing a parody of Chappell Roan's 'HOT TO GO!!' – and on 18 November 2024, Sabrina delighted fans by 'arresting' Marcello Hernández, the actor who plays Domingo, at her concert in LA.

The final installment in the Kelsey saga took place on 16 February 2025, and Sabrina herself featured as Kelsey's childhood bestie, who'd just got out of jail. She and the rest of the 'Kels squad' sang a parody of 'Defying Gravity', and then she joined the groomsmen as they performed another version of 'Espresso', which ended with Sabrina dancing exuberantly next to actor Pedro Pascal. Pure chaos.

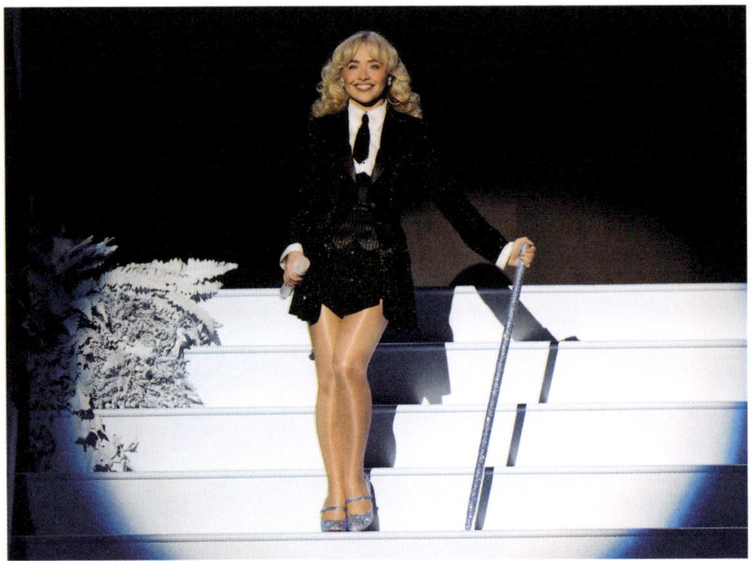

SCREAM IF YOU WANT TO WIN A GRAMMY

November 2024 saw the announcement of the Grammy 2025 nominations – and a certain five-foot-tall singer's name came up a lot. Sabrina received an amazing six nominations: Best New Artist, Album of the Year and Best Pop Vocal Album for *Short n' Sweet*, Song of the Year for 'Please Please Please', and Record of the Year and Best Pop Solo Performance for 'Espresso'.

Sabrina shared a video online showing her and her team on her tour bus, watching the nominations coming in and screaming with delight.

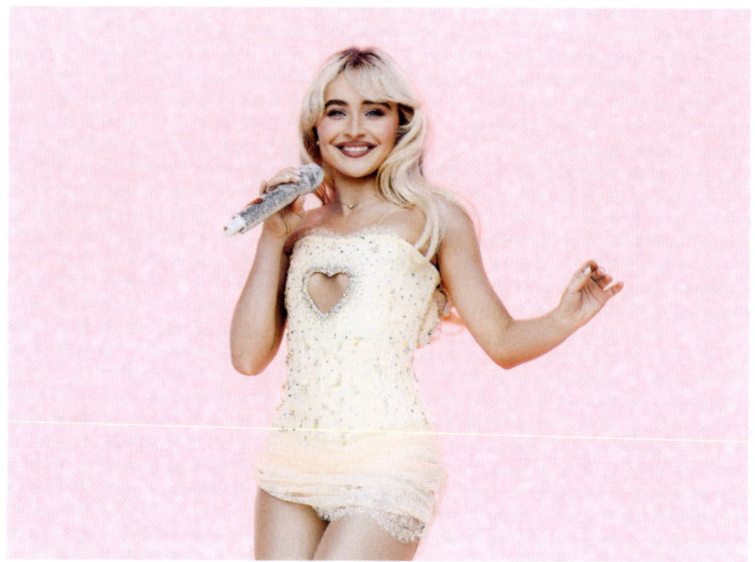

REGULAR-SIZED DESK CONCERT

On 20 December 2024, NPR released Sabrina's Tiny Desk Concert. Tiny Desk Concerts feature selected artists performing a live concert at the desk of *All Songs Considered* host Bob Boilen, and have become something of an institution – although some fans joked that Sabrina's shorter stature meant the desk wasn't all that tiny.

She wore a pale blue babydoll dress and her usual luxurious blonde curls, and delivered a set with country vibes that included 'Taste', 'Bed Chem', 'Please Please Please', 'Slim Pickins', 'Espresso' and 'Juno'.

I'M WORKING *THE LATE SHOW*

December 2024 also saw Sabrina make an appearance on *The Late Show with Stephen Colbert*. She looked elegant in a striking black blazer dress with huge gold buttons and leopard-print collar and cuffs – but when Stephen presented her with an espresso martini, she grinned and challenged him to a chugging contest.

Reflecting on her incredibly successful year, she told him: 'I feel so lucky. Singing is all I've ever wanted to do, writing songs is my favourite thing in the world. And the fact that I can do it and people listen … it [sounds] sentimental, but it's a gift, and I'm grateful.'[83]

She also explained that her dad played her 'Rocky Racoon' by the Beatles when she was very young and that she promptly fell in love with Paul McCartney. 'I was convinced he was my future husband.' As an adult, she met him in person: 'It felt like I was entering an alternate universe. Like, the Upside Down vibes – like *Stranger Things*, but a lot happier than *Stranger Things*.'

Later in the interview, she got the giggles when Colbert swore, telling him: 'They told me I can curse backstage, and I forgot because […] I came out here, and it looks like a church a little bit in here, and so I was like, "Don't curse, the Lord is upon us."'

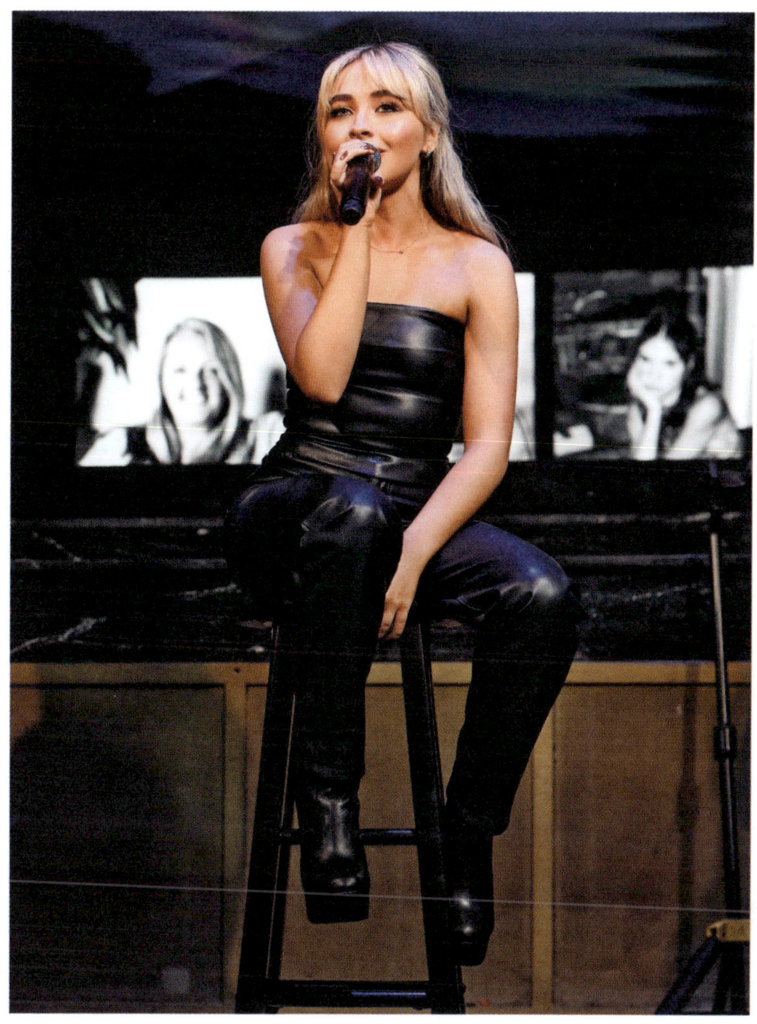

A NONSENSE CHRISTMAS

Sabrina marked Christmas 2024 with her very own Netflix special, *A Nonsense Christmas with Sabrina Carpenter*. She told *Time* magazine: 'It's an hour of literal nonsense [...] It's so fun, so chaotic.'[84]

The special featured guest stars including Shania Twain, Cara Delevingne and Kali Uchis, while Sean Astin made a special appearance as Sabrina's new boyfriend, who turns out to be Santa Claus. The show was packed with memorable moments, but the highlight had to be her duet of 'Last Christmas' with fellow pop sensation Chappell Roan, both dressed in extravagant white furry coats. The two women had had an incredible year, and it was easy to see why they'd each made such a splash.

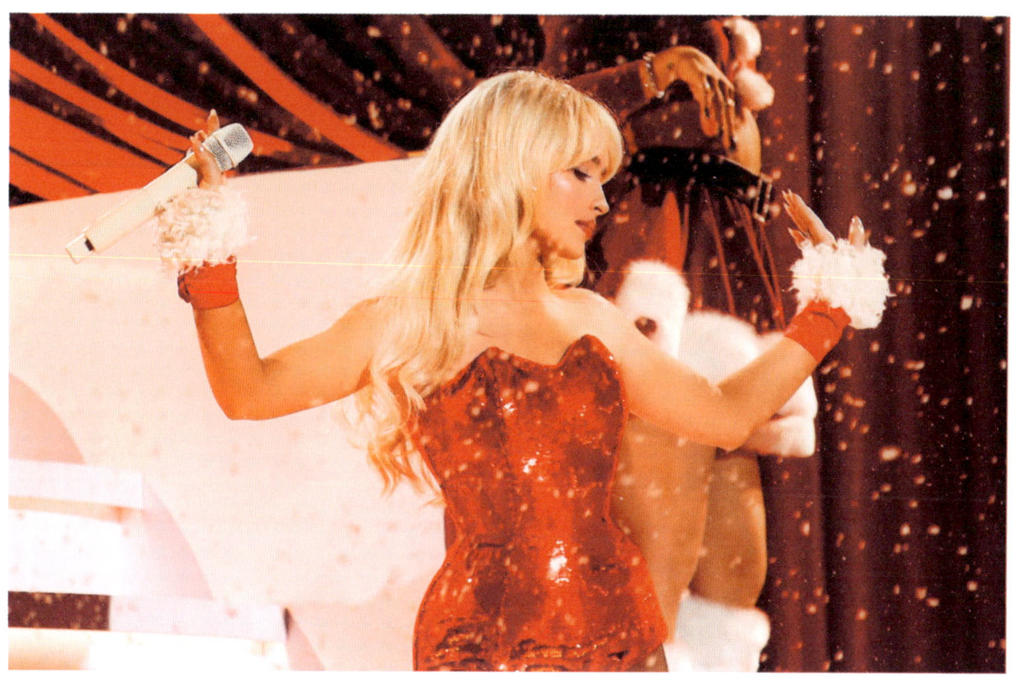

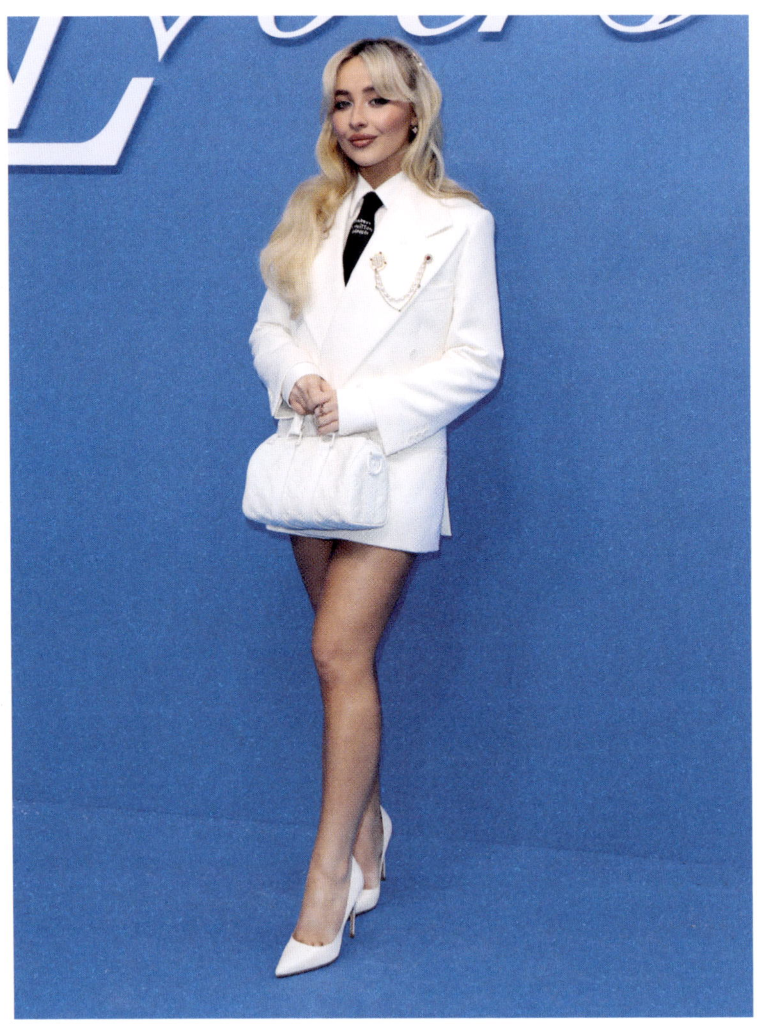

ENDING 2024 WITH A BANG

Sabrina saw out 2024 with 'Espresso' being named the number-one most-streamed song of the year on Spotify, while 'Please Please Please' also made the list, coming in at number 13. Over on Apple Music, 'Espresso' was named number three in the top songs globally for that year, and 'Please Please Please' was number 16.

Sabrina was also named the top artist on TikTok in the US, thanks to the virality of her hits encouraging TikTokers to use them in their content. In the UK, meanwhile, 'Espresso' solidified its status as one of the biggest songs of the year when it was played during the New Year's Eve fireworks display in Central London.

All this success clearly left Sabrina in a reflective mood. In an Instagram post, she mused: 'new year's resolution no more dick jokes – it's gonna be really hard.'[85]

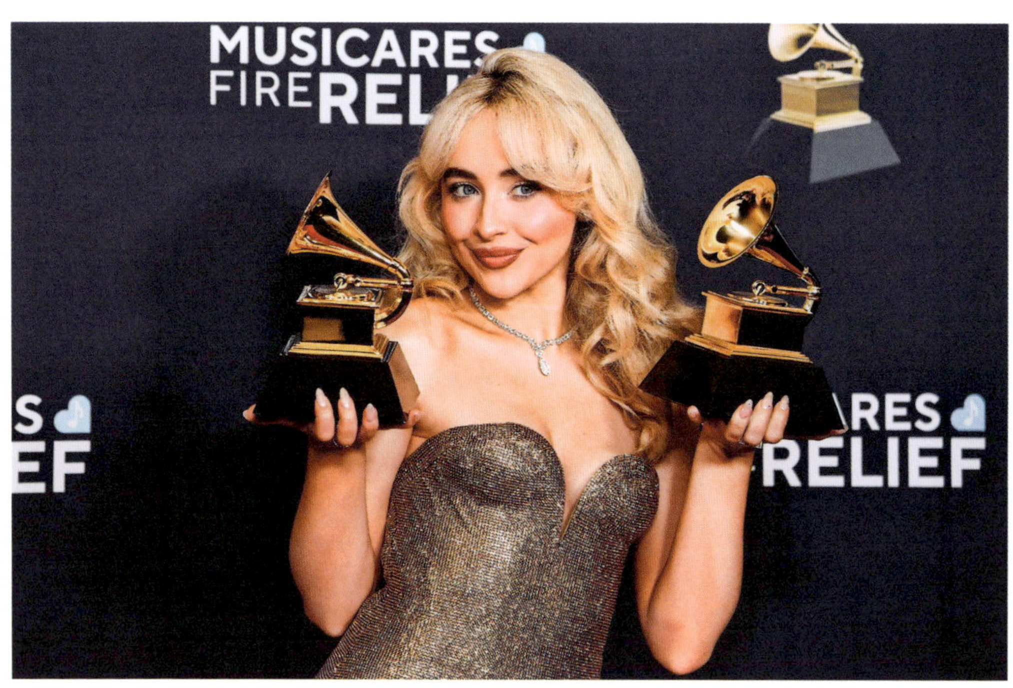
MUSICARES
FIRE RELIEF
RES
RELIEF
EF

GLOWING AT THE GRAMMYS

February 2025 saw the 67th Grammy Awards, and after her slew of nominations (see page 96), Sabrina was invited to perform. She delighted the crowd with a typically playful set during which things seemed to go wrong – but it all turned out to be her famous comic timing in action. Borrowing elements from 1978's iconic *Goldie Hawn Special*, the performance opened with Sabrina on a staircase dressed in a glittering black jacket and holding a cane, jumping about as she attempted to stay in the spotlight, which kept veering away. As she descended the steps, she began to sing 'Espresso' – and promptly disappeared into the staircase. She clambered out, continued singing, and it only got more hilarious from there, with parts of the stage collapsing and dancers falling over. Afterwards, host Trevor Noah remarked: 'That was amazing and funny, which I didn't appreciate. Really, Sabrina? You're just gonna take my job like that?'[86]

Sabrina won the Grammy for Best Pop Vocal Album, and gave a heartfelt speech thanking her fans, family, friends and team. During the speech, she worried that she might have said 'hell' too many times – and then finished with: 'Thank you, holy shit, bye.'[87]

A VERY BRIT-ISH SCANDAL

On 1 March 2025, the annual Brit Awards were held in London. Sabrina was invited to perform as the show's opener, and thrilled fans by appearing onstage to the opening chords of 'Rule Britannia!', dressed in a red sparkly military-style minidress with stockings and suspenders. She then launched into 'Espresso', followed by a steamy rendition of 'Bed Chem'. There were Union Jacks, there were dancers in red military jackets and bearskin hats – and there were 825 complaints made to media watchdog Ofcom, most of which related to a rather cheeky moment when Sabrina knelt in front of one of the 'Royal Guards' before they both disappeared under the stage. Oops.

Sabrina was nominated for International Artist of the Year and International Song of the Year – and won the Global Success Award.

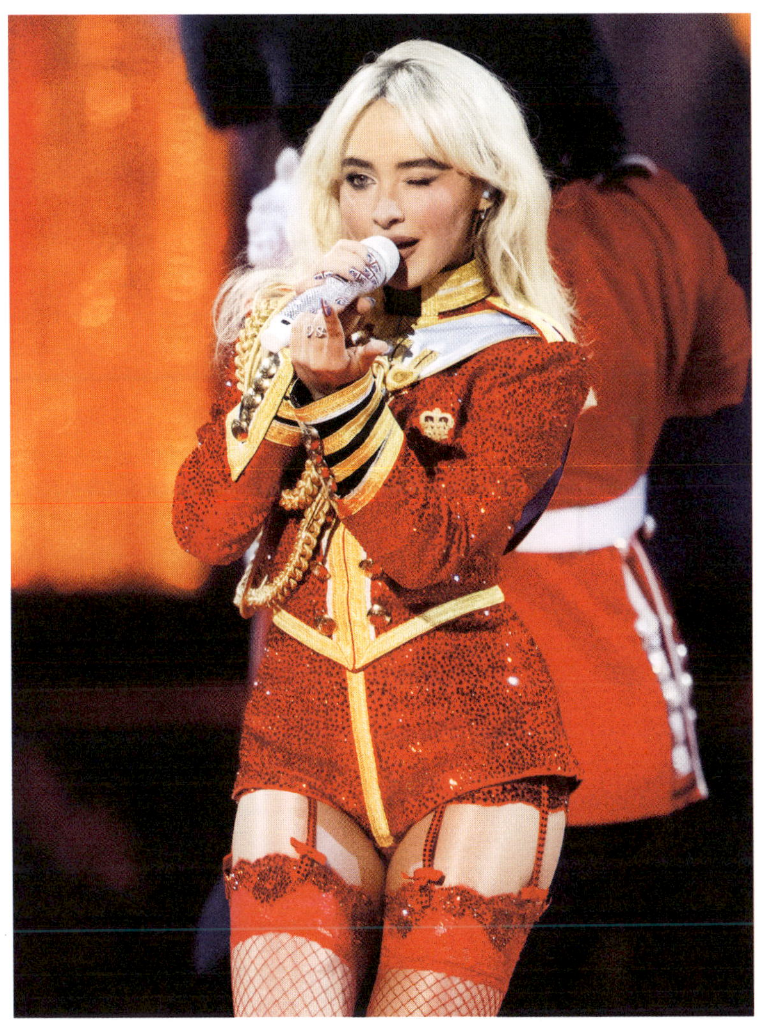

MARCHING INTO LONDON

Back in 2018, Sabrina was asked in an interview if she had any ultimate life goals, and she said: 'I'd love to sell out the O2 or Wembley; I'm not going to be picky about which one!'[88]

On 8 and 9 March 2025, she smashed that goal out of the park, playing two sold-out shows at the 20,000-capacity O2 Arena in London. As well as delighting fans on one night with a cover of 'Come on Eileen' by British band Dexy's Midnight Runners, she also adjusted her famous sparkly towel moment (see page 81) to reveal that she was wrapped in a Union Jack.

Writing on Instagram after the shows, Sabrina said: 'the last two nights at the @theo2london felt like such a little british dream, i opened there when i was 18 and it's been my goal ever since to come back and play my own shows. Then you not only sold them out but you also made my album number 1 in the UK again while I was there. What did i do to deserve ya?'

From singing cover songs in an under-the-stairs cupboard to selling out arenas, it's been a truly epic journey so far – and, as Sabrina said to *Vanity Fair* in October 2024: 'I'm truly just getting started.'[89]

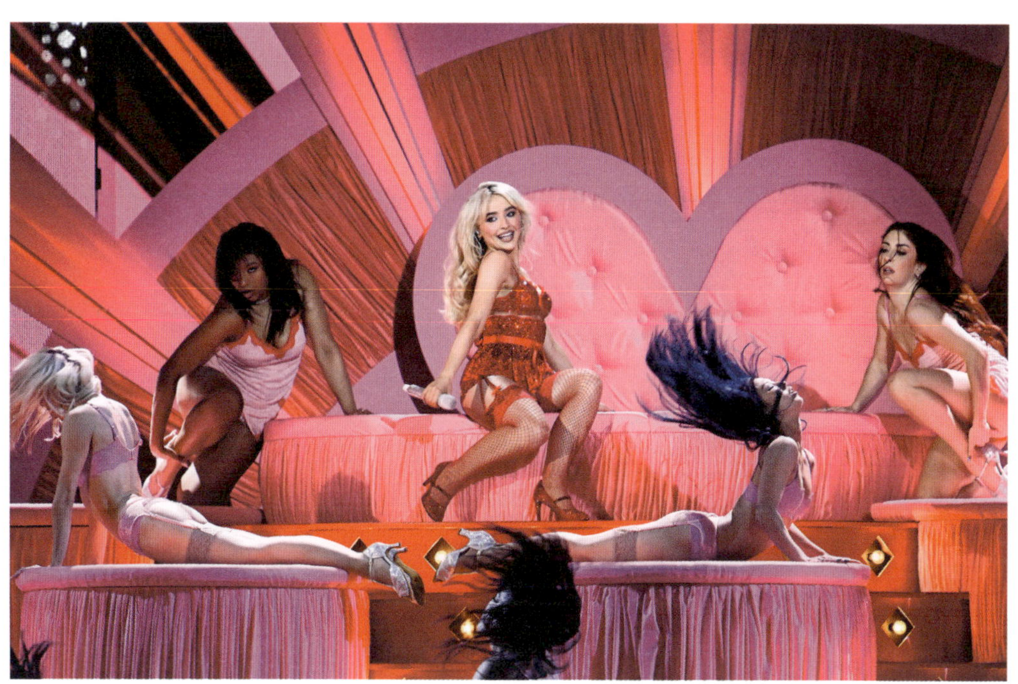

ENDNOTES

1. Huber, Eliza. 'Becoming a popstar was Sabrina Carpenter's destiny'.
2. Huber, Eliza. 'Becoming a popstar was Sabrina Carpenter's destiny'.
3. Apple Music. 'Sabrina Carpenter: Short n' Sweet, songwriting and "Espresso" | Apple Music'. Interview with Zane Lowe. YouTube, 22 August 2024. https://www.youtube.com/watch?v=enaGNnGB99I.
4. Aguirre, Abby. 'How the world fell for Sabrina Carpenter'. *Vogue*, 11 February 2025.
5. Hirschberg, Lynn. 'Sabrina Carpenter knows she has you hooked'. *W Magazine*, 5 September 2024.
6. Aguirre, Abby. 'How the world fell for Sabrina Carpenter'.
7. *W Magazine*. 'Sabrina Carpenter talks her celebrity crushes and being a child star | W Magazine'. YouTube, 5 September 2024. https://www.youtube.com/watch?v=s7HG4ntaxpM
8. Aguirre, Abby. 'How the world fell for Sabrina Carpenter'.
9. Aguirre, Abby. 'How the world fell for Sabrina Carpenter'.
10. Hawke, Maya. 'Sabrina Carpenter and Maya Hawke on rethinking the popstar playbook'. *Interview Magazine*, 8 February 2024.
11. Maoui, Zak. 'Sabrina Carpenter veers into the fast lane'. *GQ*, 25 February 2022.
12. Aguirre, Abby. 'How the world fell for Sabrina Carpenter'.
13. Hirschberg, Lynn. 'Sabrina Carpenter knows she has you hooked'.
14. Aguirre, Abby. 'How the world fell for Sabrina Carpenter'.
15. Garcia, Thania. 'Summer of Sabrina Carpenter: Hitting no. 1 on the charts, getting advice from best friend Taylor Swift and what Barry Keoghan really thinks about her lyrics'. *Variety*, 6 August 2024.
16. Huber, Eliza. 'Becoming a popstar was Sabrina Carpenter's destiny'.
17. Miller, Rude. 'Sabrina Carpenter takes on the world at Musikfest'. Lehighvalleylive.com, 13 August 2016.
18. Feldman, Lucy. 'Sabrina Carpenter has waited her whole life for this'. *Time*, 2 October 2024.
19. Aramesh, Waiss. 'Sabrina Carpenter gave us the song of the summer. She's got a plan for all seasons'.
20. Maoui, Zak. 'Sabrina Carpenter veers into the fast lane'.
21. D'Souza, Shaad. '"I'm a tyrant!" Pop superstar Sabrina Carpenter on freakish fame, fighting Disney and writing the song of the summer'. *Guardian*, 23 August 2024.
22. Aguirre, Abby. 'How the world fell for Sabrina Carpenter'.
23. Prance, Sam. 'Sabrina Carpenter talks *Singular, The Hate U Give* and the film she wants to make with Joey King'. Capitalfm.com, 21 December 2018.
24. Smith, Tracy. 'Sabrina Carpenter on "Short n' Sweet"'. CBSNews.com, 6 October 2024.
25. Garcia, Thania. 'Summer of Sabrina Carpenter: Hitting no. 1 on the charts, getting advice from best friend Taylor Swift and what Barry Keoghan really thinks about her lyrics'.
26. Feldman, Lucy. 'Sabrina Carpenter has waited her whole life for this'.
27. Hirschberg, Lynn. 'Sabrina Carpenter knows she has you hooked'.
28. Walsh, Savannah. 'That's that Sabrina Carpenter espresso'. *Vanity Fair*, 20 June 2024.
29. Kessler, Alex. 'Sabrina Carpenter is a gilded goddess in Paco Rabanne at the Met Gala'. *Vogue*, 3 May 2022.
30. Vogue. 'Sabrina Carpenter on getting ready for her first Met Gala | Met Gala 2022 with Emma Chamberlain'. YouTube, 3 May 2022. https://www.youtube.com/watch?v=EEzi4PnZPkM
31. Waheed, Jabeen. 'Sabrina Carpenter on navigating her twenties, finding her voice through music and "adding to her story" with *Emails I Can't Send* deluxe edition'.
32. Aguirre, Abby. 'How the world fell for Sabrina Carpenter'.
33. Hawke, Maya. 'Sabrina Carpenter and Maya Hawke on rethinking the popstar playbook'.
34. Waheed, Jabeen. 'Sabrina Carpenter on navigating her twenties, finding her voice through music and "adding to her story" with *Emails I Can't Send* deluxe edition'.
35. Waheed, Jabeen. 'Sabrina Carpenter on navigating her twenties, finding her voice through music and "adding to her story" with Emails I Can't Send deluxe edition'. *Glamour*, 17 March 2023.
36. Carpenter, Sabrina (@sabrinacarpenter). Instagram post, 20 August 2022. https://www.instagram.com/p/ChfVvSUJ9fF
37. Aguirre, Abby. 'How the world fell for Sabrina Carpenter'.
38. Waheed, Jabeen. 'Sabrina Carpenter on navigating her twenties, finding her voice through music and "adding to her story" with *Emails I Can't Send* deluxe edition'.
39. Feldman, Lucy. 'Sabrina Carpenter has waited her whole life for this'.
40. Feldman, Lucy. 'Sabrina Carpenter has waited her whole life for this'.
41. Aguirre, Abby. 'How the world fell for Sabrina Carpenter'.
42. D'Souza, Shaad. ' "I'm a tyrant!"
43. Aguirre, Abby. 'How the world fell for Sabrina Carpenter'.
44. Carpenter, Sabrina (@sabrinacarpenter). Instagram post, 10 November 2022. https://www.instagram.com/sabrinacarpenter/p/CkyqsyHPrrj
45. Huber, Eliza. 'Becoming a popstar was Sabrina Carpenter's destiny'.
46. Carpenter, Sabrina (@sabrinacarpenter). Instagram post, 2 June 2023. https://www.instagram.com/p/Cs_tCqtuWmL
47. Walsh, Savannah. 'That's that Sabrina Carpenter espresso'.
48. Aguirre, Abby. 'How the world fell for Sabrina Carpenter'.
49. D'Souza, Shaad. '"I'm a tyrant!"'
50. Aguirre, Abby. 'How the world fell for Sabrina Carpenter'.
51. Perry, Kevin. 'Priest stripped of duties for letting Sabrina Carpenter film music video in church'. *Independent*, 27 November 2023
52. Sabrina Carpenter. 'Sabrina Carpenter – Feather / Nonsense [Dick Clark's New Year's Rockin' Eve with Ryan Seacrest 2024]. YouTube, 3 January 2024. https://www.youtube.com/watch?v=FqBzTHOJCNU.
53. Aramesh, Waiss. 'Sabrina Carpenter gave us the song of the summer. She's got a plan for all seasons'.
54. Carpenter, Sabrina (@sabrinacarpenter). Instagram post, 24 February 2024. https://www.instagram.com/p/C3tnjYqyU1b
55. D'Souza, Shaad. '"I'm a tyrant!"'
56. Hirschberg, Lynn. 'Sabrina Carpenter knows she has you hooked'.
57. Aguirre, Abby. 'How the world fell for Sabrina Carpenter'.
58. Feldman, Lucy. 'Sabrina Carpenter has waited her whole life for this'.
59. D'Souza, Shaad. '"I'm a tyrant!"'
60. Aramesh, Waiss. 'Sabrina Carpenter gave us the song of the summer. She's got a plan for all seasons'. *Rolling Stone*, 17 June 2024.
61. Feldman, Lucy. 'Sabrina Carpenter has waited her whole life for this'.
62. Xxsusannycxx. 'sabrina carpenter – please please please [live]'. YouTube, 9 June 2024. https://www.youtube.com/watch?v=0N07ceP5Xdl
63. First We Feast. 'Sabrina Carpenter talks nonsense while eating spicy wings | Hot Ones'. YouTube, 11 July 2024. https://www.youtube.com/watch?v=msnI0D1SDSg.
64. *The Tonight Show* Starring Jimmy Fallon. 'Sabrina Carpenter talks Short n' Sweet album, Adele singing "Espresso" and Jenna Ortega'. YouTube, 23 August 2024. https://www.youtube.com/watch?v=DPO7imV0LHg.
65. *The Tonight Show* Starring Jimmy Fallon. 'Sabrina Carpenter talks Short n' Sweet album, Adele singing "Espresso" and Jenna Ortega'.
66. *The Tonight Show* Starring Jimmy Fallon. 'Sabrina Carpenter talks Short n' Sweet album, Adele singing "Espresso" and Jenna Ortega'.
67. Amelia Dimoldenberg. 'Sabrina Carpenter | Chicken Shop Date'. YouTube, 23 August 2024. https://www.youtube.com/watch?v=wEFz0gRoXxg
68. Feldman, Lucy. 'Sabrina Carpenter has waited her whole life for this'
69. *The Tonight Show* Starring Jimmy Fallon. 'Sabrina Carpenter talks Short n' Sweet album, Adele singing "Espresso" and Jenna Ortega'.
70. Feldman, Lucy. 'Sabrina Carpenter has waited her whole life for this'.
71. MTV. 'Sabrina Carpenter wins Song of the Year for "Espresso"! #VMAs'. YouTube, 12 September 2024. https://www.youtube.com/watch?v=4iiVNVBMJPw.
72. Apple Music. 'Sabrina Carpenter: Short n' Sweet, songwriting and "Espresso" | Apple Music'., 22 August 2024
73. *The Tonight Show* Starring Jimmy Fallon. 'Sabrina Carpenter talks Short n' Sweet album, Adele singing "Espresso" and Jenna Ortega'.
74. Aguirre, Abby. 'How the world fell for Sabrina Carpenter'.
75. Aguirre, Abby. 'How the world fell for Sabrina Carpenter'.
76. Feldman, Lucy. 'Sabrina Carpenter has waited her whole life for this'.
77. Aguirre, Abby. 'How the world fell for Sabrina Carpenter'.
78. Feldman, Lucy. 'Sabrina Carpenter has waited her whole life for this'.